HISTORIC ROYAL PALACES
PUZZLES & QUIZZES

✳ ✳ **SARAH WARWICK** ✳ ✳

This edition published in 2024 by Arcturus Publishing Limited
26/27 Bickels Yard, 151–153 Bermondsey Street,
London SE1 3HA

Copyright © Arcturus Holdings Limited

Produced under licence from
Historic Royal Palaces
Enterprises Limited (2024)
© Historic Royal Palaces
www.hrp.org.uk

All rights reserved. No part of this publication may be reproduced, stored in a retrieval system, or transmitted, in any form or by any means, electronic, mechanical, photocopying, recording or otherwise, without prior written permission in accordance with the provisions of the Copyright Act 1956 (as amended). Any person or persons who do any unauthorised act in relation to this publication may be liable to criminal prosecution and civil claims for damages.

AD011711UK

Printed in the UK

✳✳ CONTENTS ✳✳

Introduction 5

Puzzles 7

Solutions 139

INTRODUCTION

THE PALACES
Historic Royal Palaces is an independent charity formed in 1998 to look after six awe-inspiring palaces. These are:
- The Tower of London – famed fortress and prison on the banks of the River Thames.
- Hampton Court Palace – the grand home of Henry VIII and all six of his wives.
- Banqueting House – famous for its Rubens ceiling and being the site of Charles I's execution.
- Kensington Palace – the birthplace of Queen Victoria and a residence for royals for over 300 years.
- Kew Palace – the intimate and beloved family home of King George III and Queen Charlotte.
- Hillsborough Castle – a grand country house, Northern Irish royal residence, and home of the Secretary of State for Northern Ireland.

Each of these extraordinary properties is packed with history, treasures, art and stories – all waiting to be discovered by you through this wonderful collection of puzzles and quizzes.

THE PUZZLES
Inside you'll find an array of wordsearches, quizzes, crosswords and mazes, all inspired by the fascinating buildings listed above. Most of these are easily solved and you'll get the hang of them in no time.

WORDSEARCHES
Your task is to find the hidden words running backwards and forwards, up and down, or diagonally in both directions. In some puzzles, only the underlined words need to be found.

CROSSWORDS

Solve the clues and fill in the grids. Alongside each grid is a clue related to the Historic Royal Palaces. Once you have completed the grid, unscramble the letters in the shaded squares and reveal the answer.

QUIZZES

Put your knowledge to the test or discover something intriguing and new with these themed quizzes on an array of fascinating topics related to the Historic Royal Palaces.

MAZES

Imagine yourself at Hampton Court Palace as you find your way to the centre of these puzzles.

Prepare to follow in royal footsteps as you enter the fascinating world of the Historic Royal Palaces. What will you discover inside?

1   The Tower of London

The Tower of London is a historic castle on the River Thames. It was first founded as part of William the Conqueror's fortifications of London, to secure his position after his victory at the Battle of Hastings.

1. What kind of birds are associated with the Tower?

2. What is said will happen if these birds ever leave?

3. In 2023, the Tower welcomed a new chick, named in tribute to the new king. What is his name?
    a. Rex   b. Charles   c. Carol

4. Yeoman Warders were given a popular nickname because of their high consumption of what?

5. Which type of spirit is every Yeoman Warder sent on his or her birthday?

6. The Yeoman Warder's uniform shows the king's special cypher displaying which initials?

7. The last person to be executed in the Tower was a Nazi spy. What was his name?
    a. Willem Weiss   b. Tomas Turm   c. Josef Jakobs

8. Name the three queens of England who were executed on Tower Green.

9. Guy Fawkes was also interrogated here. In what year was his 'Gunpowder Plot'?
    a. 1595   b. 1605   c. 1615

Queen Victoria

```
L K M U E L O S U A M G D P Y
E C C M B U C K I N G H A M Y
O I O O O V S E T N R L K S I
P R C S B W R H G H H E S I E
O E A H B I O I Y C N E G E R
L D R N P O E D K S R Y L A D
D E R M G R R E I P N I M L R
H R E Z E E N N M W B S T B A
C F V V E T G E E U G V T E W
R Y O R M T O F J A U P Z R D
A S N R O H A S T I N G S T E
N H A N E L C E S P A N I E L
O M H S U C C E S S I O N A W
M T N A T S E T O R P D K C T
W N Z V A L E X A N D E R N X
```

- ALBERT
- ALEXANDER
- BRITISH EMPIRE
- BUCKINGHAM PALACE
- DUKE OF KENT
- EDWARD
- EMPRESS
- FREDERICK
- GOLDEN JUBILEE
- HANOVER
- HASTINGS AFFAIR
- KENSINGTON SYSTEM
- KING LEOPOLD
- MONARCH
- OSBORNE HOUSE
- PRINCE OF ORANGE
- PROTESTANT
- RAMSGATE
- REGENCY
- ROYAL MAUSOLEUM
- SOVEREIGN
- SPANIEL
- SUCCESSION
- WIDOW OF WINDSOR

3 Hampton Court Palace

Originally an ordinary manor house, Hampton Court was purchased in 1514 and transformed into an extraordinary palace.

1. Name the Archbishop of York who bought Hampton Court in 1514.

2. In 1528, the newly expanded palace was given to Henry VIII in a vain attempt by its owner to stay in the king's favour. It soon became his favourite home, but out of how many?
   a. 25   b. 43   c. 60

3. When Henry took over the palace in order to provide 'bouche of court' for up to 450 courtiers twice a day, the king needed to quadruple the size of what?
   a. Kitchens   b. Dining halls   c. Banqueting tables

4. Henry VIII installed an astronomical clock, which didn't just show the time and date but also the current tide level at London Bridge. Why was this important?
   a. Food deliveries   b. Defences   c. Travel

5. The Great Hall was used for plays, such as when James I's court spent Christmas and New Year 1603–04 at the palace to escape an outbreak of what?
   a. Smallpox   b. Typhoid   c. Plague

6. On that occasion, it is believed that William Shakespeare's 'King's Men' first performed which two famous one-word-title plays for the new Stuart king?
   a. *Hamlet* and *Macbeth*   b. *Othello* and *Macbeth*
   c. *Hamlet* and *Othello*

7. In 1647, Charles I found himself under house arrest at Hampton Court after his defeat in which war?

8. Who was the last monarch to reside in the palace?
   a. George I   b. George II   c. George III

4 Maze

Start at the top and find a path to the middle of the maze.

5 Royal History – 1066

1. When Edward the Confessor died, the throne was taken by one Harold Godwinson, who is also known by what title?
   a. Harold I   b. Harold II   c. Harold III

2. There were two other claimants to the English throne: the first was William, Duke of... which region of France?

3. The other was Harald Hardrada, who was king of which country?
   a. Sweden   b. Denmark   c. Norway

4. Before moving on to fight William, Harold and Harald met at which battleground?

5. During the Battle of Hastings, how did William's Norman soldiers trick the English ones?
   a. They hid inside a wooden horse
   b. They pretended to run away
   c. They bribed them

6. Before the battle, what appeared in the sky that was later believed to herald William's victory?
   a. The sun   b. A full moon   c. Halley's comet

7. What happened to Harold during the battle?

8. On what famous textile is the fate of Harold sewn?

9. Harold's mother Gytha Thorkelsdóttir came to William the Conqueror pleading for her son's body by offering what in exchange?
   a. Her hand in marriage
   b. Harold's body weight in gold
   c. Her first daughter in marriage

10. William was crowned king at Westminster Abbey on which date?
    a. 31st October 1066   b. 5th November 1066
    c. 25th December 1066

6 Hillsborough Castle – History

- ANTE ROOM
- BANQUET
- BIG HOUSE
- CHURCH OF ST MALACHY
- CIVIL RIGHTS MOVEMENT
- COURTHOUSE IN THE SQUARE
- DUKE OF ABERCORN
- BENJAMIN FRANKLIN
- GOOD FRIDAY AGREEMENT
- GOTHIC
- HILL FAMILY
- MAGENNIS FAMILY
- MO MOWLAM
- OPERATION BANNER
- PARTITION
- PEACE PROCESS
- PRINCESS ALICE
- QUAKERS
- QUEEN ELIZABETH II
- ROAD TO MOIRA
- ROYAL RESIDENCE
- SILVER JUBILEE
- STATE DRAWING ROOM
- THE FORT

7 Kew Palace

First built as a fashionable mansion in 1631, Kew Palace is the smallest of the royal palaces.

1. Samuel Fortrey, for whom the palace was built, was a merchant of what?
   a. Silk   b. Cotton   c. Wool

2. Confusion over Fortrey's nationality and a particular style of gable led to the building being known as the...
   a. Flemish House   b. Dutch House
   c. French House

3. How did the house first come into royal possession in 1728?
   a. It was leased   b. It was won   c. It was gifted

4. In what year did the royal family actually buy it?
   a. 1731   b. 1781   c. 1831

5. George III and his wife Queen Charlotte had many happy times at Kew during their first 25 years of marriage. They would play duets on which two instruments?
   a. Harpsichord and pianoforte
   b. Harpsichord and flute
   c. Flute and pianoforte

6. How many children did they have together?
   a. 5   b. 10   c. 15

7. Two of George III's sons, Princes William (later William IV) and Edward, took part in what double ceremony at Kew Palace on 11th July 1818?

8. Queen Elizabeth II celebrated her birthday in 2006 with a family dinner party at Kew Palace. How old was she?

8 Crossword

Royal house succeeding the Stuarts

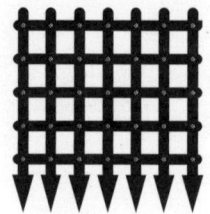

Across

1. Sea foam (4)
3. Israeli monetary unit (6)
5. Reproductive cells (3)
6. Ursine mammal (4)
7. Free-and-easy (6)
9. Having no bearing on or connection with the subject at issue (10)
14. Popular drink (3)
15. Be of service (3)
17. Gratification of another's desire or humour (10)
20. Things of value or usefulness (6)
22. Reign (4)
23. Very warm (3)
24. Make up one's mind (6)
25. Flexible pipe for conveying a liquid (4)

Down

1. Give in (6)
2. Compel (5)
3. Pouch (3)
4. Stretchy fabric (7)
8. Expanse of salt water (3)
10. Print anew (7)
11. Dashed (3)
12. Long and slippery fish (3)
13. Grandmother (3)
16. Cut or eliminate (6)
18. Female deer (3)
19. Home planet (5)
21. That girl (3)

9   Palace Lives – The Princes in the Tower

The 'Princes in the Tower' mysteriously disappeared in 1483.

1. Name the 12-year-old boy king who disappeared.
   a. Edward V   b. Richard III   c. William II

2. When the boys' father Edward IV died in 1483, his brother Richard had the princes taken to the Tower for what alleged reason?

3. What happened before the boy king could be crowned?

4. Who became king instead?
   a. Harold III   b. George I   c. Richard III

5. Sir James Tyrrell, a faithful servant of the new king, is said to have confessed to what before he was executed for treason in 1502?

6. Who was the boys' older sister who went on to marry Henry VII, uniting the houses of Lancaster and York?

7. In what year did workmen at the Tower of London find a wooden box containing two small human skeletons?
   a. 1574   b. 1674   c. 1774

8. An urn designed by Sir Christopher Wren marks the resting place of the putative princes in which abbey?

9. In 1789, two more child skeletons were found near Edward IV's coffin, which are other potential remains of the princes. Where are they?
   a. Westminster Abbey   b. Hampton Court Palace
   c. St George's Chapel, Windsor

10. Whose skeleton was found under a car park in Leicester in 2012?

10   Palace Lives – Thomas Cromwell

Thomas Cromwell was born in 1485 in Putney. A self-made man, he eventually served as chief minister to Henry VIII.

1. What did Cromwell's father do for a living?
       a. Blacksmith   b. Merchant   c. Painter

2. Cromwell became a statesman after securing the patronage of Henry VIII's chief minister. What was his name?

3. After his patron's downfall, Cromwell found favour with the king by helping him with what problem?
       a. The church   b. His divorce   c. His finances

4. After he helped bring down Anne Boleyn, Cromwell engineered a marriage between Jane Seymour's sister Elizabeth and who else?
       a. Himself
       b. His son, Gregory
       c. His son, Henry

5. A pious man, what did Cromwell pay for so that all of Henry VIII's subjects had ready access to God's word?

6. Cromwell also arranged Henry's ill-fated marriage to his fourth queen. What was her name?

7. Although Henry forgave Cromwell for organising his disastrous fourth marriage, Cromwell's enemies convinced the king that his minister was plotting against him. What happened to Cromwell?

8. Which book, published in 2009, detailed the life and times of Thomas Cromwell, turning him into an unlikely hero?

9. Cromwell's great, great grand-nephew, born in 1599, also played a seismic role in the political and religious life of the country. Name him.

11 The Tower of London – The Crown Jewels

```
E P N S C V G N A N I L L U C
G V Q K R L W N A J K G O I E
A O S I O U F I I O J E T C O
S L L W J L Y H R P R N S M
S G E I N A T I L I G I G H W
U C Z N G F N C A C R H K Y B
O V E E I O E L L P U P C R G
P E R P O P U Y L M D P O U C
E L U R T F S B U G R A E S O
R V S T L R G U P L A S M A R
J E A S E U E R M V W N E E O
K T P B W M E D A I D O R R N
G A R N E T B B O A E O A T E
D L O G J U A X V O T P L M T
Y E L S R E N N Y K S S D J H
```

- AMPULLA
- CORONET
- CROWN
- CULLINAN
- DIADEM
- EMERALD
- GARNET
- GOLD
- JEWEL
- KOH-I-NOOR
- KYNNERSLEY
- ORB
- PRINCE
- REGALIA
- REPOUSSAGE
- RING
- RUBY
- SAPPHIRE
- SCEPTRE
- SPINEL
- SPOON
- ST EDWARD
- TREASURY
- VELVET

12   Palace Lives – The Six Wives of Henry VIII

1. Henry VIII met how many of his wives while they were ladies in waiting to his other wives or daughters?
        a. 2   b. 3   c. 4

2. To whom was Katherine of Aragon married for five months in 1501, eight years before she married Henry?

3. On what basis did Henry claim, when he wanted to get rid of her, that their marriage had never been legitimate?

4. His marriage to Katherine was annulled in May 1533. When did he marry Anne Boleyn?
        a. January 1533
        b. June 1533
        c. January 1534

5. How many days did the king wait after Anne Boleyn's death before marrying Jane Seymour?
        a. 11   b. 15   c. 21

6. How long was Anne of Cleves married to Henry VIII?

7. She was 24 when they married – how old was the king?
        a. 36   b. 48   c. 60

8. Why were Thomas Culpeper and Francis Dereham convicted of treason and executed on 10th December 1541?

9. What is the name of the award-winning 2017 musical by Toby Marlow and Lucy Moss that retells the lives of the six wives of Henry VIII?
        a. *Wives*   b. *Six*   c. *Henry*

13 Crossword

Agricultural epithet of George III

Across

1 Sprang (5)
3 Berkshire town, famous for its racecourse (5)
7 Rich and elaborate cake (6)
9 Spreads seeds (4)
10 Vehicle that carries people and equipment to the scene of a conflagration (4,6)
14 Office of a bishop (3)
16 Suffer with or like another (10)
19 Steal goods, take as spoils (4)
20 Enclose (6)
22 Prickle, barb (5)
23 Little-used side road (5)

Down

1 Exit a computer (3,3)
2 Food in a pastry shell (3)
4 Japanese rice dish (5)
5 Duty (4)
6 Domesticated cavy (6,3)
8 After the expected time (5)
11 Clairvoyance (inits) (3)
12 Acquire (3)
13 Lacking experience of life (5)
15 In a mild, soft manner (6)
17 Measuring device (5)
18 Secret scheme (4)
21 Put into words (3)

14   Royal Dynasties – The House of Normandy

The Normans ruled England from 1066 to 1154, starting with William I and ending with Stephen.

1. William I was the founder of the Tower of London and also the deviser of the first census of England's lands in 1086. What was it called?

2. The Conqueror's crown passed to his second son, William II, who was known as Rufus – why?

3. William II died in which forest, which had been established as royal hunting grounds by his father?
   a. New Forest
   b. Sherwood Forest
   c. Royal Forest of Dean

4. Sir Walter Tyrrell, who shot Rufus by accident, fled to France but not before doing what?
   a. Marrying the king's daughter
   b. Going to the blacksmith
   c. Stealing some gold

5. William I's fourth son, Henry I, took the throne in 1100 after his brother's death. He was known as Henry Beauclerc, which means what?
   a. 'Good scholar'   b. 'Good clerk'   c. 'Good son'

6. After Henry I's only legitimate son was killed, England experienced a period of civil war fought between which two rivals for the throne, both grandchildren of William I?
   a. Stephen and Matilda
   b. Robert and Rebecca
   c. James and Jennifer

7. How was this war known?
   a. The English Civil War
   b. The Seven Years' War
   c. The Anarchy

15 Banqueting House – History

- ANJOU
- PRINCE HENRY'S BARRIERS
- MASQUE OF BEAUTY
- JEANNE DE GONTAUT
- ANTOINE DE NOAILLES
- DYNASTY
- FESTIVITIES
- FREDERICK
- LEONARD FRYER
- GEORGE GOWER
- RAPHAEL HOLINSHED
- INCINERATE
- ORLANDO GIBBONS
- BISHOP JUXON
- LEWIS LIZARD
- LONDON LOOP
- POCAHONTAS
- REVELRY
- ROBERT STICKELLS
- SUPREME HEAD
- TOMOCOMO
- UNION OF THE CROWNS
- ANTHONY VAN DYCK

16   Kensington Palace

Kensington Palace was the birthplace of Queen Victoria and has been home to members of the royal family for over 300 years.

1. When first bought by royals William III and Mary II for their private London residence in 1689, the original house shared the name of which town in the Midlands?
   a. Coventry   b. Stratford   c. Nottingham

2. Plans for expanding the house into a grand palace were designed by which contemporary architect?

3. Mary II is said to have started which interiors trend?
   a. Displaying family photos in the toilet
   b. Painting woodwork with glossy paints
   c. Throw cushions

4. In which room did William III catch a chill that would lead to his death in 1702?
   a. The antechamber   b. The King's Gallery   c. His bedroom

5. The Queen's State Apartments, including the Queen's Gallery, were designed for Mary II. What items did she display there?
   a. Her jewels   b. Her miniature collection
   c. Her Chinese and Japanese porcelain collection

6. After William and Mary's deaths, Mary's sister Queen Anne was next to live at Kensington with her husband, who was Prince of which Scandinavian country?
   a. Denmark   b. Sweden   c. Norway

7. Name the 'greenhouse' built for Queen Anne in 1704–05 for housing plants in winter and hosting parties in summer?

8. What is the name of the boating lake in Kensington Gardens that was commissioned by Queen Caroline in the 1720s?

9. Who was the last monarch to live at Kensington Palace, dying there during his breakfast on 25th October 1760?
   a. George I   b. George II   c. George III

17 Crossword

Sarah Churchill's husband, Duke of ___

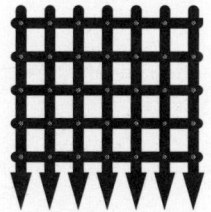

Across

1 Bottle that holds oil or vinegar for the table (5)
3 Greek island (5)
6 Ridge of rock, coral etc (4)
8 Sleeping compartments on a ship (6)
10 Aqualung (5)
12 Adipose (5)
14 Manufactured, not occurring naturally (3-4)
15 Greek letter (5)
16 Brightly coloured seashell (5)
18 Sloping kind of handwriting (6)
19 Unwanted plant (4)
20 Impurities left in the final drops of a liquid (5)
21 James ___, author of *Ulysses* (5)

Down

1 Popular game played with pieces of stiffened paper (5)
2 Imp (3)
3 Exposed surface in a mine (8)
4 Being (9)
5 Short formal piece of writing (5)
7 Determine the amount of (9)
9 Yellow songbirds often kept as pets (8)
11 Item of equipment used in baseball (3)
13 Fuss (3)
15 Two-sixths (5)
17 Fence made of shrubs (5)
19 Which person? (3)

18   Royal History – The Birth of Edward VI

Edward VI was the desperately longed-for son and heir of Henry VIII. Henry is said to have wept with joy upon first holding his infant son.

1. On 12th October 1537 at Hampton Court Palace, Edward VI was born. Which of Henry VIII's wives was the boy's mother?
   a. Jane Seymour   b. Anne of Cleves   c. Katherine Parr

2. How many rounds of ammunition were fired from the Tower of London as wild celebrations broke out in cities and villages across the country?
   a. 1,000   b. 1,500   c. 2,000

3. How many days after Edward's birth did his mother die of post-birth complications?

4. Once he had been weaned, all of the prince's food was…
   a. Boiled   b. Certified organic
   c. Tested by a servant before being given to him

5. What did Edward own that provided entertainment outside of lessons?

6. Henry was determined to keep his son (who he referred to as 'this whole realm's most precious jewel') at Hampton Court, away from London's maladies. What happened to any servant who fell ill?
   a. Put into isolation   b. Fired   c. Sent away

7. Despite all this effort, in 1541 Edward fell ill with which disease?
   a. Malaria   b. Yellow fever   c. Diphtheria

8. Edward shared his lessons with his constant companion, Barnaby Fitzpatrick. What happened when Edward misbehaved?

19   **Maze**

Start at the top and find a path to the middle of the maze.

20   The Tower of London – Infamous Prison

```
M D D K V D E D A E H E B Y E
X R R W E K S A R A C K E A L
L A A Y S E L C A N A M J R O
Z W B E O C B I A O N T F K P
O O M R X G N A I T Q R R X C
F H A G G J B T L E L A U U W
S J L P O R T C U L L I S E N
A C F V E X T K L E I T A R E
A T A A G Q N T I K F O E E R
N M W V W Y D G W S Y R L V U
E B A B E K H B L D C W G E T
W E F L O N E A F Q E U S D R
O N O I E N G S A D R A W N O
H B L O O D Y E H A N G E D T
L P Q U A R T E R E D Z L F C
```

- ANNE ASKEW
- JOHN BALLIOL
- BEHEADED
- BLOODY
- ANNE BOLEYN
- DRAWN
- ROBERT DEVEREUX
- GUY FAWKES
- RANULF FLAMBARD
- LADY JANE GREY
- HANGED
- CATHERINE HOWARD
- KRAY
- MANACLES
- NICHOLAS OWEN
- MARGARET POLE
- PORTCULLIS
- QUARTERED
- RACK
- SIR WALTER RALEIGH
- SCAVENGER
- SKELETON
- TORTURE
- TRAITOR

21   Palace Lives – William the Conqueror

The first Norman king, William I, or William the Conqueror, was the son of Robert I, Duke of Normandy.

1   Conquering was clearly in William I's blood – his great-great-great-grandfather Rollo was what kind of warrior?

2   William set his eye on Matilda of Flanders for his bride, but she initially refused him. Why?
    a. He was too short   b. He was illegitimate
    c. He was already married

3   William founded the Tower of London after the Battle of Hastings, as he was narvous of what?

4   What does the White Tower house today?
    a. The Crown Jewels
    b. The Royal Armouries collections
    c. The ravens

5   The White Tower is a classic example of a what – the name given to large towers in castles that were fortified residences?

6   Apart from some decorative limestone imported from Normandy, the tower was made with Kentish ragstone, quarried in thin pieces from which Kent town?
    a. Maidstone   b. Canterbury   c. Folkestone

7   In what year did UNESCO award the Tower of London world heritage status for being 'the most complete example of an 11th-century fortress palace remaining in Europe'?
    a. 1978   b. 1988   c. 1998

8   After building the Tower, William moved to cement his power by 'Harrying the North', a brutal campaign to subjugate Northern England. The latter led to what percentage of Yorkshire's population either dying or emigrating?
    a. 35 per cent   b. 55 per cent   c. 75 per cent

22 Hillsborough Castle – Gardens

```
P G K U S D N U O R G Z Q U M
E I M E A D O W S N M O S O H
A I I Q M K F L O W E R S L W
R Q I H X U E V P Y N S C O E
M I D M T A T L D A F D K I N
A N T I H E S E I P P O P R O
I Y E W M Q B S N H V X E I Y
N P R D F Z S A D I Z D Y S L
E E A Y R O K N Z E P K I E S
L O G I O A E R E I L A P S E
P N R E O P G K X D L L L X W
M I A P E X A U V R C E A D O
E E M T E L L I V N A R G W B
T S A Q C N J E E R T E M I L
B U T C H E R D N A L D O O W
```

- BLOODY BUTCHER
- BLUE NEPETA
- EARL OF GRANVILLE
- ESPALIER FRUIT TREES
- FLOWERS
- GRANVILLE GARDEN
- IRISES
- KILKENNY PEARMAIN
- LADY ALICE'S TEMPLE
- LADY ROSE BOWES-LYON
- LAKE
- LIME TREE WALK
- MEADOWS
- MOSS WALK
- ORIENTAL POPPIES
- ORNAMENTAL GROUNDS
- PEONIES
- PINETUM
- PRINCESS MARGARET
- QUEEN ELIZABETH II
- STATUE OF OSSIAN
- THE WALLED GARDEN
- WOODLAND
- YEW TREE WALK

23   The Tower of London

1. The oldest part of the Tower of London is a Norman building dating back to the time of William I. It is called the White Tower – why?

2. The White Tower has four turrets. What shape are they?

3. Why did Leonora Cohen attack the Crown Jewels in 1913?

4. Which of these is not a former use of the Tower moat?
        a. Allotment   b. Campsite   c. Prison

5. The moat is an example of a fosse. What does the word 'fosse' mean?

6. Apart from flooding, the moat has been dry since 1845. Why was it drained?

7. The Tower was home to a Royal Menagerie for over 600 years. In 1252, Henry III was given what cold-weather animal by the King of Norway (which was let out on a chain to swim and fish in the Thames)?
        a. Polar bear   b. Penguin   c. Seal

8. Edward I created a new home for the Menagerie at the western entrance to the Tower, which became known as what?

9. One of its ostriches died in the 1750s because people were trying to check a theory that the birds could digest what?
        a. Bones   b. Nails   c. Shoes

10. Where did the animals go when the Royal Menagerie closed in 1826?

24　　　　　　　　　　Maze

Start at the top and find a path to the middle of the maze.

25   Royal Dynasties – The House of Plantagenet

The House of Plantagenet was a royal dynasty originating in France.
The Plantagenets ruled England from 1154 to 1485.

1   The name 'Plantagenet' is said to have originated because Geoffrey V, Count of Anjou, father of the first Plantagenet king, had a habit of wearing what?
    a. A yellow broom flower in his helmet
    b. A sprig of lavender in his buttonhole
    c. A sprig of rosemary in his belt

2   Henry II was the first Plantagenet king. He assumed the throne in 1154, and also ruled parts of which country?
    a. France   b. Belgium   c. Spain

3   Henry II's son, Richard I, acquired what nickname due to his noble, brave and fierce leadership?

4   Richard's brother and heir was so unpopular a king that he was forced to sign the Magna Carta at Runnymede, limiting the power of the monarchy forever more. His name?
    a. Jack   b. John   c. James

5   Henry III's crest is still used today to represent England in sporting events. Which three animals are featured on it?

6   In the mid-14th century, what disease swept across England, killing between 40–60 per cent of its population, including Edward III's daughter Joan?

7   Edward III's oldest son, Edward of Woodstock, was killed in battle in 1376. What was his nickname, given for the colour of his armour or his reputation as a fearsome soldier?

8   Edward III's grandson, Richard II, took the throne next. What major uprising did he quell in 1381?

26 King George II

- ACT OF SETTLEMENT
- AHLDEN HOUSE
- AUSTRIAN SUCCESSION
- BATTLE OF DETTINGEN
- BRITISH MUSEUM
- CAROLINE OF ANSBACH
- COMMONS
- GENERAL ELECTION OF 1747
- GOTTINGEN
- HAMPTON COURT PALACE
- HANOVER
- JACOBITES
- KING'S COLLEGE
- LEICESTER HOUSE
- LORDS
- PRINCE OF WALES
- PROVINCE OF GEORGIA
- QUEEN ANNE
- REGENCY BILL
- SEVEN YEARS' WAR
- SOUTH SEA BUBBLE
- THE HAGUE
- WESTMINSTER ABBEY
- WHIGS

27 Hillsborough Castle

Hillsborough Castle began as a grand family home and is now the official home for Northern Ireland's secretary of state and a royal residence.

1 Not technically a castle, Hillsborough is typical of what kind of mansion owned by the Anglo-Irish after the 1600s?

2 Until the 1600s, the Hillsborough estate was owned by the Magennis family, whose descendants went on to develop which iconic Irish product?
    a. Kerrygold   b. Guinness   c. Baileys

3 The estate passed on to Sir Moyses Hill, who had joined the army to seek his fortune in Ireland. He arrived in Ireland with which military leader, a famous favourite of Queen Elizabeth I?
    a. Earl of Essex   b. Earl of Sussex   c. Earl of Wessex

4 By the 1650s, the Hill family estate stretched for how many miles?
    a. 110   b. 130   c. 150

5 Wills Hill, Earl of Hillsborough, hosted which American founding father at Hillsborough in 1771?
    a. George Washington   b. Thomas Jefferson
    c. Benjamin Franklin

6 In 1925, the castle was bought from the Hill family by the British government to be the residence of the Governor of Northern Ireland. How much did they pay?
    a. £24,000   b. £54,000   c. £74,000

7 Between the 1920s and the 1970s, the castle was the official residence of the Governors of Northern Ireland, and was known as what?

8 In 1934, a portion of the castle was destroyed by a fire started by a careless guard who dropped a lit cigarette on the roof while doing what?
    a. Lowering a flag   b. Replacing a tile
    c. Saluting a fly-past

9 In March 1946, which young woman made her first solo royal visit, staying at Hillsborough Castle with her aunt and uncle who was the Governor?

28 Crossword

Banqueting House architect (2 words)

Across

1 Luxurious country residence (5)
3 Marie ___, chemist who discovered radium (5)
7 Diplomacy (4)
9 Distant but within sight (6)
11 Aquatic creature (5)
13 Measuring stick (5)
14 Fop (5)
15 Alcoholic brew (3)
16 Dirt-free (5)
17 Affect with wonder (5)
20 Punctuation mark : (5)
22 Stabbing weapon (6)
23 Beehive State of the USA (4)
24 Tall perennial grasses (5)
25 Denim trousers (5)

Down

1 Elector (5)
2 Espresso coffee with milk (5)
4 No longer needed or useful (9)
5 Ahead of time (5)
6 Colouring agent (3)
8 Workmate (9)
10 Difficult experience (6)
12 Dreamlike state (6)
16 Durable aromatic wood (5)
18 Small rodent (5)
19 Distinctive spirit of a culture (5)
21 Source of metal (3)

29   Royal History – The Gunpowder Plot

The Gunpowder Plot of 1605 is the well-known attempt to assassinate the king by Guy Fawkes and his fellow conspirators. It is still commemorated to this day.

1. In which northern city was Guy Fawkes born in 1570?
   a. Newcastle   b. York   c. Chester

2. Which building did he and his fellow conspirators plan to blow up?

3. Which king were they trying to assassinate?

4. There were 13 conspirators in total. What was their religion?

5. Guy Fawkes was found guarding 36 barrels, approximately 2,500 kg of gunpowder. This would have completely destroyed everything within what radius?
   a. 20 metres   b. 40 metres   c. 60 metres

6. Where were the conspirators taken for interrogation?

7. To what three-part fate were Fawkes and eight others sentenced?

8. After the plot was discovered, suspicion of those of the same religion as the conspirators led to the rigorous enforcement of the recusancy law – but what was it?

9. What tradition, begun by royal decree, do the British follow to commemorate the foiling of the Gunpowder Plot?

10. What 2005 film focuses on a masked freedom fighter, played by Hugo Weaving, who wears a Guy Fawkes mask?

30   Hampton Court Palace

1. Henry VIII spent three of his honeymoons at Hampton Court Palace, and married which of his wives there on 12th July 1543?

2. The ghost of which other of Henry VIII's wives is said to appear on the Silverstick Stairs on the anniversary of her son's birth in October each year?

3. What is now known as the Haunted Gallery in the Tudor Apartments is said to be inhabited by the screaming ghost of yet another wife. Name her.

4. That gallery is lined with portraits of Henry VIII and his family, including one of his mother. What was her name?

5. One of the pictures, *The Family of Henry VIII*, shows the king with his wife, Jane Seymour, and his three children, Mary, Elizabeth and Edward, painted in 1545 when the latter was eight. What is strange about this?

6. Sybil Penn, who was a servant to four Tudor monarchs, is said to appear in the palace as a ghost, the 'Grey Lady'. Which spotty medieval disease did she succumb to?

7. Mary I also spent her honeymoon at Hampton Court Palace. To whom was she married?

8. First hung in the Great Hall in 1546, Henry VIII commissioned a series of tapestries, woven in Brussels from wool, silk, and gold and silver thread, showing scenes from the life of which Biblical patriarch?
   a. Adam   b. Abraham   c. Aaron

9. How many tapestries did Henry VIII own?

10. Famously an art fan and founder of the Royal Collection, which king used the palace to house much of his notable art collection, including Mantegna's *The Triumphs of Caesar* paintings?
    a. James I   b. Charles I   c. John

Banqueting House – Architecture

```
C I T C E L C E Z K K A R E
E A R B V C H B I T R S M B Q
Z N A E B O C A J J E O U Y P
E P A L L A D I A N Y C Y E M
I R P L A T N E M G E S D B N
R U E F L X R H N X R I A A
F S L X H C Y O R O M Y F L I
D T F C D I T E Y E M E I U H
P I L F Y N H A N P S A R S T
S C E N I O L T T T S G A T N
W A M H V I S O O H P R S R I
A T I I S E N O T S A L A A R
G E S T R Z N O Y B B J V D O
S D H E T A N I T A L A P E C
E N T A B L A T U R E G O X U
```

- ASHTON COURT
- BALUSTRADE
- BRYMPTON D'EVERCY
- CORINTHIAN
- DOUBLE CUBE
- ECLECTIC
- ENTABLATURE
- FESTOON
- FLEMISH MANNERIST
- FRIEZE
- HINTON HOUSE
- FRANCIS HOLLES
- IONIC
- JACOBEAN
- PALATINATE
- PALLADIAN
- PEDIMENTS
- ROYALIST
- RUSTICATED
- SEGMENTAL
- NICHOLAS STONE
- SWAGS
- VASARI
- YORK PLACE

32   Queen Victoria

Born at Kensington Palace, Princess Victoria was only fifth in line to the throne. By the time she was 18, she was queen.

1. Queen Victoria's actual first name was what?
       a. Elizabeth   b. Charlotte   c. Alexandrina

2. Victoria spent her childhood summer holidays in which coastal town, which was given the unique status of 'Royal Harbour' by King George IV in 1820?
       a. Hastings   b. Tenby   c. Ramsgate

3. During her lifetime, the queen is said to have written more than 60 million words, mostly in what?
       a. Poetry   b. Novels   c. Diaries

4. She and Prince Albert bought which house on the Isle of Wight as a holiday home for their family?

5. After Albert's death in 1861, Victoria became close to her Highland manservant, and their relationship became the subject of which 1997 film starring Judi Dench?

6. Victoria was no feminist, saying that the idea of giving what to women was a 'mad and wicked folly'?

7. Victoria was pronounced Empress of India in 1877, and was so committed to her role that she asked her servant Abdul Karim to teach her which language?
       a. Hindi   b. Urdu   c. Gujarati

8. Did Victoria ever visit India?

9. Queen Victoria was known as the 'Grandmother of Europe', but how many grandchildren did she have?
       a. 24   b. 36   c. 42

10. In 1901, Victoria died isurrounded by her family, including her grandson, Wilhelm II, King of Prussia – also known to us by what name?

33 Crossword

The Wars of the Roses rivals, the Yorkists and the ___

Across

- 4 Water flow resulting from sudden rain or melting snow (5)
- 7 Former (3-4)
- 8 In a higher position (5)
- 10 Fake jewellery (5)
- 12 Be victorious (3)
- 13 Association organised to promote art, science or education (9)
- 17 Took in solid food (3)
- 19 Prickly desert plants (5)
- 22 Interlace (5)
- 23 On the way (2,5)
- 24 Swift, quick (5)

Down

- 1 Utilising the energies of the sun (5)
- 2 Fame, celebrity (6)
- 3 ___ *Night*, Christmas carol (6)
- 4 Ooze (4)
- 5 Tori ___, singer whose albums include *American Doll Posse* (4)
- 6 Young of an eel (5)
- 9 Pay a call on (5)
- 11 Extremely sharp (5)
- 14 Tastelessly showy (6)
- 15 Drinking vessel (6)
- 16 Happen (5)
- 18 At no time in the past or future (5)
- 20 Pouch in a bird's gullet where food is stored (4)
- 21 Decorated with frosting (4)

34   Royal Dynasties – The House of Lancaster

A branch of the House of Plantagenet, the House of Lancaster was first formed by the creation of the Earldom of Lancaster in 1267.

1. The first king of the House of Lancaster was Henry IV. Who was his father, one of Edward III's sons?

2. In 1399, while the reigning King Richard II was in Ireland, Henry Bolingbroke sparked a populist uprising and declared himself King Henry IV. In which London Palace did he imprison Richard?
    - a. The Tower of London
    - b. St James's Palace
    - c. Greenwich Palace

3. Where did Richard II die, probably from starvation?
    - a. Pontefract Castle
    - b. The Tower of London
    - c. Westminster Abbey

4. His son Henry V went on to inherit the throne. After the battle of Agincourt in 1415, Henry V also claimed the throne to which other European nation, although he was never crowned?

5. In 1422, his son Henry VI was the youngest person ever to assume the throne. How old was he?
    - a. 8 months   b. 8 years   c. 18 years

6. Shakespeare's plays *Richard II*, *Henry IV (Part 1)*, *Henry IV (Part 2)* and *Henry V* are collectively known as what?

7. The House of Lancaster was one of the two royal houses that fought the Wars of the Roses. What was the other?

8. What was the first battle of the Wars of the Roses?
    - a. The Battle of Stevenage
    - b. The Battle of Biggleswade
    - c. The Battle of St Albans

9. At that battle, Richard of York defeated the Lancastrians and imprisoned Henry IV, but as the saying goes, he 'gave battle in vain' as he never became king himself. Why was this?

35 Kensington Palace – The Jewel Room

```
S G N I R R A E M E R A L D D
E K K T N E M A I L R A P Y E
M G I G H C A U P Z H T Y E R
N N N T X C Z R Y V T Y A S F
A I H I C D O P A R U R E I L
I N S F R H N O J U D S E U A
R E O N B F I F R N C B D O A
O T K Q Z P A N A B M N W L G
T S O Q Q R Y X G X M O A R A
C I K J A R E H T A E F R O R
I R P D T L E W W Y D E D M R
V H C W A Q B Q W D A L V A A
N C S O U T H E S K I C I N R
I Y R A M V Q N R I D Q I O D
N W O R C F I F E T W V K V R
```

- ALBERT
- ALEXANDRA
- ALFRED
- AMAZONIA NECKLACE
- CHRISTENING
- CROWN JEWELLER
- DIADEM
- DIAMOND BROOCH
- EARL OF SOUTHESK
- EMERALD
- FEATHER HEADDRESS TIARA
- FIFE TIARA
- FRINGE TIARA
- GARRARD COUTURE
- KING EDWARD VII
- JOSEPH KITCHING
- KOKOSHNIK TIARA
- LOUISE
- OPENING OF PARLIAMENT
- PARURE
- PENDANT EARRINGS
- QUEEN MARY
- QUEEN VICTORIA
- ROMANOV COURT

36 The Tower of London

1. The Tower of London's Medieval Palace (the name by which St Thomas's Tower, the Wakefield Tower and the Lanthorn Tower are known) was created by Henry III and his son Edward I. In which century did they both start their rule?
    a. 11th b. 13th c. 15th

2. The chapel in the Wakefield Tower is associated with which king who died in 1471 while a prisoner in the Tower during the Wars of the Roses?

3. Following historic custom, whenever a Royal Naval vessel moors on the Tower Wharf, the Captain must present the Constable of the Tower with the 'Dues'. What are these?

4. A carving of the Dudley coat of arms can be found in the Beauchamp Tower, attributed to John Dudley who was imprisoned at the Tower in the aftermath of his father's unsuccessful plot to put who on the throne?

5. What was the name of the water gate through which state prisoners often entered the Tower?
    a. Traitors' gate
    b. Treason gate
    c. The black gate

6. The ceremonial locking of the fortress each night has become known as what?

7. For how many years was the Tower used as a prison?
    a. Over 600 b. Over 800
    c. It has always been a prison

8. In what decade did the Tower cease being a prison?
    a. 1840s b. 1890s c. 1950s

37 Crossword

Dutch artist who painted Princess Mary as the goddess Diana (2 words)

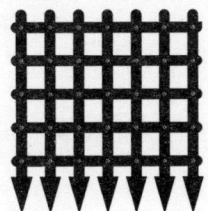

Across
1. Edible part of a nut (6)
6. Counting frame (6)
7. Shared online journal (4)
8. Using a needle and thread (6)
10. Ring-shaped bread roll (5)
13. Slanted letters (7)
16. Popular board game (5)
18. Solution (6)
20. Scottish island, capital Portree (4)
21. Exceptional creative ability (6)
22. Shelled aquatic reptile (6)

Down
1. Skewered meat dish (5)
2. Solid lump of a precious metal (6)
3. Young woman (4)
4. Obstruction of one heavenly body by another (7)
5. Symbol of victory (1-4)
9. Long narrative poem (4)
11. Chinese herb believed to have medicinal powers (7)
12. Interweave (4)
14. Drink to follow immediately after another drink (6)
15. Emblem worn like a brooch (5)
17. Strainer (5)
19. Remainder (4)

38   Palace Lives – Edward I

Edward I and his father Henry III were responsible for creating the Tower of London we know today, expanding William I's fortress.

1. Edward created a concentric castle at the Tower of London. What does this mean?

2. Despite it being his official residence, Edward I only stayed at the Tower of London for how many days in his 35 years of rule?
        a. 53 days   b. 83 days   c. 113 days

3. A modern re-creation of his bed can be found in St Thomas's Tower today. It's size is fitting for a tall, imposing king who was known as what?
        a. Largelegs   b. Longshanks   c. Tall Ted

4. Which money-making institution was permanently established at the Tower during Edward's reign?

5. The first part of Edward's reign was spent subduing the Welsh and building a series of castles in Wales. Which Welsh leader did he defeat?
        a. Dafydd ap Llywelyn
        b. Owain Glyndwr
        c. Llywelyn ap Gruffudd

6. His son, later Edward II, was born at Caernarfon Castle in 1284 and later given which title?

7. After conquering Scotland in 1296, Edward ordered that the ancient Stone of Scone, upon which the kings of Scotland were crowned, should be moved where?

8. Which Scottish leader did Edward capture in Robroyston in 1305 and have hanged, drawn and quartered?

9. Edward died in 1307, on his way to fight which other Scottish leader?

39 Maze

Start at the top and find a path to the middle of the maze.

40 The Tower of London – Yeoman Warder

```
V T A L X W H Y R T N E S T A
K K G D A C A H R L I F F U R
K X L O R I A R R A T H J H G
C H Q A Q M N G R H C C N K N
Z I E V L H S O H A H Q O K M
W S N E E A O K M T N Y R P T
N F T U L E R U C E S T E E N
J S P U T U X U E O R D M L A
D X T S T D D E A S R E A T E
K E Y S R N L Z E N E M C S G
M G D A O G T Y A E D O A I R
E J U C U Y Z T R V R F R H E
E G E B O N N E T A A S I T S
T E S N U S R S I R W Y O H J
R E L B A T S N O C G O M Z Q
```

- BONNET
- BUGLE
- CEREMONIAL
- CONDUCT
- CONSTABLE
- DUES
- GUARD
- HALT
- HAMLETS
- KEYS
- MOIRA CAMERON
- RAVENS
- RUFF
- SALUTE
- SEARCH
- SECURE
- SENTRY
- SERGEANT
- SHAMROCK
- SUNSET
- THISTLE
- TUNIC
- WARDER
- WARRANT

41 Palace Lifestyles – Hobbies and Habits

1. Which king was known for his campaigns against tobacco smoking? His *A Counterblaste to Tobacco* (1606) was one of the first anti-smoking pamphlets.

2. Which queen was a patron of a number of pigeon racing societies, in recognition of her interest in the sport?
    a. Elizabeth I   b. Victoria   c. Elizabeth II

3. The vast art collection of which Stuart king forms the basis for the Royal Collection?

4. Although his son is more famous for his sporting (and other) exploits, which king made tennis popular across his realm?

5. Who gained the nickname 'Farmer George' because of his keen and scholarly interest in agriculture?

6. 'Whether he's hedge-laying in the pouring rain, striding, like a mountain goat up impossibly steep Highland hills… or pruning at Highgrove, this is where he finds true peace.' Who said this, describing Charles III's love for outdoor life?

7. Which monarch was an avid stamp collector and honorary vice-president of what became the Royal Philatelic Society of London?

8. What was Queen Mary an avid collector of, which are now housed in the British Museum?
    a. Books   b. Christmas cards   c. Menus

42   Hillsborough Castle

- BEEHIVES
- BURIAL GROUND
- CRANNOG
- DINING ROOM
- DRAWING ROOM
- GAS WORKS MEADOW
- GEORGIAN HOME
- GROTTO
- HIDDEN PINETUM
- HOUNDS
- HYDRO HOUSE
- ICE HOUSE
- IMAGINARY MENAGERIE
- LADY ALICE'S TEMPLE
- LADY GREY'S STUDY
- RED ROOM
- ROBIN TRAIL
- SHELL HOUSE
- STAIR HALL
- STATE ROOMS
- THRONE ROOM
- WALLED GARDEN
- WESTON PAVILION
- WILLOW HOUSE

43 Royal Dynasties – The House of York

A branch of the House of Plantagenet, three members of the House of York would be kings of England.

1. The House of York eventually won the crown, when it was taken by Richard of York's son Edward IV in the bloody Battle of Towton, in which year?
    a. 1461   b. 1481   c. 1501

2. Edward IV had a great library and encouraged learning. It was during his reign that William Caxton established what in the outbuildings of Westminster Abbey?
    a. Printing press   b. Library   c. Art gallery

3. Why did Edward's secret marriage to one Elizabeth Woodville enrage his advisors?
    a. They were related
    b. She was not a royal
    c. She was not English

4. In fact, chief advisor Richard Neville, Earl of Warwick, was so angry he staged a revolt and reinstated Henry VI as king, leading the Earl to be given what nickname?
    a. The kingmaker
    b. The treacherous
    c. The betrayer

5. In 1465, Elizabeth Woodville re-founded which Cambridge College (originally founded by Lancastrian Queen Margaret of Anjou in 1448)?

6. Richard III (the last king of the House of York) was portrayed by Shakespeare as having which physical deformity?
    a. A club foot
    b. A harelip
    c. A hunchback

7. In which battle did Richard III lose his crown, and his life?
    a. The Battle of Bosworth Field
    b. The Battle of Bosworth Hill
    c. The Battle of Bosworth Bridge

44   Maze

Start at the top and find a path to the middle of the maze.

45   Banqueting House

Banqueting House is the magnificent last surviving complete building of a lost royal palace.

1. Name the palace that Banqueting House was originally part of.

2. Banqueting House shares an architect with the Queen's House in Greenwich. Name him.

3. The site of the palace was originally the London home of the Archbishops of York, known as York Place, but it was confiscated by Henry VIII from which Archbishop?

4. Henry VIII expanded it greatly, with plenty of sporting grounds, including a bowling green, real tennis court and a pit for cockfighting. The site of the cockfight pit would be at 70 Whitehall today: what is there now?

5. The palace was then the principal London home for the royals during the Tudor and Stuart dynasties until 1698, when what happened?

6. Who was executed outside Banqueting House on 30th January 1649?
    a. Charles I   b. James I   c. Charles II

7. On the day before Good Friday from the 13th to the 19th centuries, a ceremony was performed in Banqueting House where the monarch would distribute what?

8. They would also wash which body parts of their subjects?
    a. Their feet   b. Their hair   c. Their faces

46 Hampton Court Palace – Architecture and History

```
D H I N B C R E I T R U O C Y
K R O W K C I R B O U D Q B R
U A W O Y E S L O W J D Q A T
N I A T N U O F N Z I B O S N
S R E L L A T I P S O H G R U
N S E M E B I P I A N O V E O
E E Z G A U F A R A D A Y L C
H S J R R Z Q V M B A S E I G
C S W R E N E O O A S S D E I
T E C V D H K U R O D I E F B
I D W T O O C L D A C N R G B
K D I M X H L E Y O B N O C O
Q O E Z E X R H X T Z E J C N
M G R F H E N R I E T T A J S
I P X Y R M U I G O L O R O H
```

- BAROQUE
- BASE COURT
- BAS RELIEF
- BOUCHE OF COURT
- BRICKWORK
- COUNTRY HOUSE
- COURTIER
- GIOVANNI DA MAIANO
- MICHAEL FARADAY
- FOUNTAIN COURT
- GRINLING GIBBONS
- TWELVE GODDESSES
- GREAT KITCHENS
- HENRIETTA MARIA
- HOME PARK
- HOROLOGIUM
- KNIGHTS HOSPITALLER
- MAZE
- PIANO NOBILE
- REREDOS
- TENNIS COURT
- TUDOR
- CARDINAL WOLSEY
- SIR CHRISTOPHER WREN

47 Royal History – The Interregnum

The Interregnum began in 1649 when Charles I was executed, and ended in 1660 when Charles II was returned to the throne.

1 Charles I remains the only English monarch to have been tried and executed. Of what crime was he found guilty?

2 What did he plead during the trial?
    a. Not guilty   b. Guilty   c. He did not enter a plea

3 Charles was unpopular for many reasons, including his refusal to allow anyone except his wife to do what in his presence?
    a. Speak   b. Stand   c. Sit

4 On the morning of his execution, he requested an extra what?
    a. Hour for confessional   b. Servant
    c. Shirt

5 What title did Oliver Cromwell take as ruler of the Commonwealth in 1653?

6 What was Cromwell's religion (an extreme type of Protestantism)?

7 Cromwell's rise to power led to the banning of which winter festival, a deeply unpopular move?

8 What nickname was given to Oliver Cromwell's son Richard when he inherited his father's role as Lord Protector?

9 What name was given to the period when Charles II reclaimed the throne and re-established the monarch?

10 After Charles II returned to England, what did royalists do with Oliver Cromwell's body?

48 Crossword

1st Marquess of Downshire (2 words)

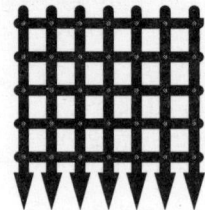

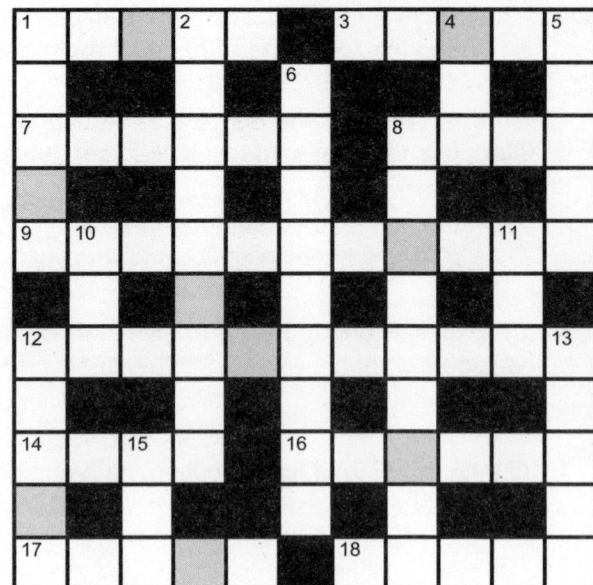

Across

1. Mediterranean island, capital Valletta (5)
3. Deviating from the truth (5)
7. Furrow (6)
8. Ban or prohibition (4)
9. Pile of decaying vegetation for use in the garden (7,4)
12. Rules governing the use of public roads (7,4)
14. Spring up (4)
16. Finger-shaped cream cake (6)
17. End resistance (5)
18. Male bee (5)

Down

1. Wizardry (5)
2. Vessel for transporting soldiers (9)
4. Decorate with frosting (3)
5. Bring together, assemble (5)
6. Swayed towards a course of action (9)
8. Relating to wheeled forms of transport (9)
10. Sash worn by Japanese women as part of traditional dress (3)
11. As well as (3)
12. Red-berried shrub much used in wreaths (5)
13. Lofty nest of a bird of prey (5)
15. Time period (3)

49 Royal Dynasties – The House of Tudor

The House of Tudor succeeded the House of Plantagenet in 1485. They reigned for more than 100 years.

1. In 1485, who was the last king of England to win his throne on the field of battle, becoming the first Tudor on the throne?

2. Despite fighting on the Lancastrian side in the Wars of the Roses, the Tudor family actually hailed from Penmynydd. Where is Penmynydd?

3. Henry VII married Elizabeth of York, a political move that brought the houses of York and Lancaster together. This was symbolised by which flower?

4. Their second son, Henry VIII, became king next. He was best known for having six wives, but how many of those wives did he have beheaded?

5. On 12th October 1537, Henry VIII's only son and heir Edward VI was born at which palace?

6. After Edward died, there was a short-lived reign of his cousin, Lady Jane Grey. For how many days was she on the throne?
    a. 7   b. 9   c. 11

7. Mary I was next. Her reign was characterised by such brutal treatment of Protestants that she got what nickname?

8. Who was the last of the Tudors, ruling for 44 years and known as the Virgin Queen?

9. In what year did the Tudor period come to an end?
    a. 1583   b. 1603   c. 1623

50   Palace Lives – Mary I

Born in 1516, Mary was Henry VIII's first legitimate child, and for a long time his only child. As a result, she received many of the royal prerogatives normally reserved for the king's heir.

1. In 1525, Mary was given her own court based at which Welsh castle?
       a. Ludlow   b. Caerphilly   c. Cardiff

2. Mary took the throne aged 37, and immediately organised her marriage to her cousin Philip. He was heir to the throne of which country?
       a. Portugal   b. Spain   c. France

3. Owing to the English law of *jure uxoris*, Queen Mary's Marriage Act was passed, meaning that Philip could only be King of England until when?

4. At her instigation, the Second Statute of Repeal was also passed, restoring England's religious position to that of 1529, complete with Papal authority. This brought back the right to try Protestants for which crime?
       a. Heresy   b. Treason   c. Witchcraft

5. After this, Mary became known for her burning of Protestants. Approximately how many 'Marian Persecutions' (as they were known) were there in all?
       a. 100   b. 300   c. 500

6. Which popular nursery rhyme is allegedly based on Mary's burning of the Oxford Martyrs: Thomas Cranmer, Nicholas Ridley and Hugh Latimer?

7. Those who weren't burned weren't safe from Mary's wrath. Which of her family members did she imprison in the Tower of London in 1554?

8. After Mary died in 1558, her much-loved husband wrote to his sister:
       a. 'I was beyond heartbroken.'
       b. 'My life will never be the same.'
       c. 'I felt a reasonable regret.'

51 Kew Palace

```
G K Y V M R Y H D O C T O R S
C E T M S E E L A I R M D T W
O R O I N U H T S N S M Q N F
N Y B R C U H U S Y O K U E N
S A U O G S M P D E L V E G O
O B Z O T E T O L Z C T E E I
R N T R T A I R Z O U R N R T
T R E X H A N V E A D G O Q U
S E L A W D Y Y U L R A M W L
E Y Y T Z Q U L F F I T J W O
N H I J E H B C O S I T E Q V
R P N X P S C G H R K K Z K E
E G G Z V T T A N Y A X Y I R
I C I M S R S V B S I S W B A
V P N D N A R I C H M O N D K
```

- ADOLPHUS FREDERICK
- ARTS
- BACH
- BOTANY
- FRANCES BURNEY
- CHARLOTTE OF WALES
- CHRISTMAS TREE
- CONSORT
- DOCTOR'S COMMONS
- DUCHY
- ERNEST AUGUSTUS
- FRENCH REVOLUTION
- GEORGE IV
- HANOVER
- KEW GARDENS
- LYING-IN HOSPITAL
- MOZART
- MUSIC
- QUEEN
- REGENT
- RICHMOND
- ROYAL WORCESTER
- STRELITZIA REGINAE
- SIR HERBERT TAYLOR

52   Sophia Duleep Singh

Princess Sophia Duleep Singh was the daughter of the deposed Maharaja Duleep Singh. She was granted Faraday House, then part of the Hampton Court Estate, as a grace and favour residence.

1. Where was the Maharaja Duleep Singh's palace until he was deposed?
   a. Kashmir   b. Lahore   c. Peshawar

2. Princess Sophia Duleep Singh is best known as a suffragette and campaigner for women's rights. Who was her godmother?

3. Sophia's childhood home was at Elvedon Hall in which English county?

4. In November 1901, Sophia took part in a demonstration in Westminster, which became known by what name, because of the abuse the women received?
   a. Black Monday   b. Black Friday   c. Black Sunday

5. 'As women do not count, they refuse to be counted. I have a conscientious objection to filling up this form.' What was Sophia Duleep Singh referring to in 1911?

6. Sophia was also a member of the Women's Tax Resistance League (WTRL), whose motto was 'No vote, No tax!' When some of her jewellery was confiscated after she refused to pay taxes, what did fellow members of the WTRL do?
   a. Attacked the bailiffs in the street
   b. Threw away their own jewellery in sympathy
   c. Bought the pieces at auction and gave them back to her

7. Like her father, Sophia supported the Lascars Club, which supported who?
   a. Indian soldiers   b. Indian seamen   c. Indian farmers

8. Despite having many interests, particularly travel, music and dog showing, what did Sophia list as her only interest in the 1934 edition of *The Women's Who's Who*?

53 Crossword

Type of burial ground in Hillsborough Castle gardens

Across

1. Firework that burns with a fizzing noise (5)
4. Plant fibre used to make rope (5)
7. Shrub that yields coffee beans (7)
8. Stiff bristle on an ear of barley (3)
9. Conduits used to convey liquids or gases (5)
11. Southern US breakfast dish (5)
12. Area of open or forested country (5)
14. Lads (5)
16. Social insect (3)
17. Hair cleanser (7)
19. Familiar by-form of the name Henry (5)
20. Curt, brusque (5)

Down

1. Musical notation indicating one half-step higher than the note named (5)
2. Large nation (initials) (3)
3. State of extreme happiness (5)
4. Informal language (5)
5. Enduring strength and energy (7)
6. Golf course by the sea (5)
10. Large flat dish used for food (7)
12. Furious indignation (5)
13. Covered with a layer of fine powder (5)
14. Shore of a sea (5)
15. Plain dough cake, often griddled (5)
18. Equality (3)

54 The Tower of London

1. The Channel 5 TV show *Inside the Tower* revealed many little-known facts, including a toilet built for which notorious figure when it was thought he could be kidnapped and imprisoned here during World War II?

2. Another episode included a dachshund puppy called Reggie, named after which infamous gangster who spent time in the Tower for refusing National Service in 1952?

3. When Queen Elizabeth II died, there was an official gun salute at the Tower with how many rounds?
    a. 70   b. 96   c. 23

4. What is the name given to the tradition, still held every three years on Ascension Day, that involves hitting the boundary markers of the Tower with sticks?

5. What does Ascension Day commemorate in the Christian faith?

6. Samuel Pepys was imprisoned for six weeks in 1679 for piracy and treason, but what do we know him best for today?

7. How many prisoners were tortured at the Tower?
    a. 11   b. 48   c. 167

8. 'They put my wrists into iron gauntlets... My arms were then lifted up and an iron bar was passed through... they left me hanging by my hands and arms fastened above my head.' What instrument of torture is being described here?

9. Many people know about the rack, a medieval tool for stretching victims, but what was the machine called that did the opposite, compressing or contorting them?

55 Hillsborough Castle

```
T D F R W S E G D I R T R A P
F A M I L Y H I T H R O N E W
Z Z A T R F N X I N E E W M N
W M R Q O I R D A G M S S O C
Z A Y H N R S O P X A E T O T
T D Z G U R G H M T G S R R G
E L E L Y O Y Q I N N K D E
R X R A K H V R X I E B H E O
R Y S U R C I P W Q H Y F R R
A I V E R S A I L L E S B P G
C W K Y T S G L B I B L E R E
E M Z S U O L R A M S A Y O I
L L A H I I S E L R A H C Y V
Z T B L H F M F C M S O C A A
X I C C I R H A W K I N G L J
```

- CHARLES II
- WINSTON CHURCHILL
- DEAD HARE AND PARTRIDGES
- DINING ROOM
- DOWNSHIRE FAMILY
- HAWKING PARTY
- IRISH BIG HOUSE
- KING GEORGE IV
- WILLS HILL
- PETER LELY
- PRINCESS MARY
- SATIRISTS
- SIR ALLAN RAMSAY
- GEORGE ROMNEY
- STAG HUNT AT VERSAILLES
- STATE ENTRANCE HALL
- STUDIO OF SEBASTIANO RICCI
- THE BIBLE
- THE RED ROOM
- THE ROYAL COLLECTION
- THE SCHORR COLLECTION
- THE SOUTH TERRACE
- THE THRONE ROOM
- JAN WEENIX

56   Palace Lifestyles – Elizabethan Beauty

1. Elizabeth I underwent a lengthy and painstaking beauty regime every single day of her 44-year reign. Why was it important for the monarch to remain looking youthful?

2. Elizabeth's entire face, neck and hands were painted with ceruse in order to achieve a fashionably pale complexion. What was ceruse?

3. Ironically, what did this concoction do to the skin?

4. Elizabeth was known for wearing a wig after her hair began falling out. How many wigs did she have?
       a. 30   b. 50   c. 80

5. Stibnite powder mixed with fat to make a paste was used as an eye-liner. By what name is this more commonly known today?

6. 'Two newly laid eggs and their shells, burnt alum, powdered sugar, borax and poppy seeds ground with water'. For what was this an Elizabethan recipe?
       a. Health drink   b. Cleansing fluid   c. Emetic

7. Elizabeth's lips and cheeks were coloured with a red paste made from beeswax, cochineal and plant dye. What is cochineal?

8. Later in her life, how did Elizabeth disguise the fact that her teeth had fallen out?
       a. Clumps of fabric
       b. False teeth made of ivory
       c. Pieces of wood, studded with gold

9. For a moisturiser, the queen used a curd made as a by-product of posset. What is a posset?

10. When bright eyes with dilated pupils became a trend, women would put drops of what in their eyes?
        a. Hemlock   b. Belladonna   c. Digitalis

57 Crossword

Original name for the Palace of Whitehall (2 words)

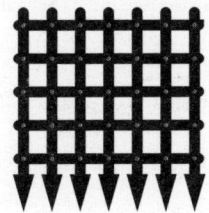

Across
1. Lever operated with the foot (5)
3. Implied (5)
7. Sickness (6)
9. Three thousand and six hundred seconds (4)
10. For, in favour of (3)
12. Somewhat ill (10)
15. Slumber (colloquial) (3)
17. Unrestrained by convention or morality (10)
20. Profound emotion inspired by a deity (3)
21. Ballet dancer's skirt (4)
22. Thoroughfare (6)
24. Devoid of clothing (5)
25. Of great weight (5)

Down
1. Writing implement (6)
2. Pompous fool (3)
4. Distinctive spirit of a culture (5)
5. Hoop that covers a wheel (4)
6. Pleasure (9)
8. Inappropriate, not justified (5)
11. Strong cord (4)
13. Turn or place at an angle (4)
14. Dodge (5)
16. In a tidy and ordered way (6)
18. Measuring instrument (5)
19. Knock senseless (4)
23. Regret (3)

58 Royal History – The Glorious Revolution

The 'Glorious Revolution' is the title given to the 1688 coup that dethroned the Catholic king in favour of Protestants William III and Mary II.

1. Which king was dethroned by William III and Mary II?

2. This event has also been known as 'the last successful invasion of England', as William III was a citizen of what country?
    a. Belgium   b. The Netherlands   c. Romania

3. What did many people at the time believe that the Catholic king would attempt to do?

4. However, his Catholicism had been mostly tolerated until what?
    a. He started preaching
    b. He brought the Pope to England
    c. He had a son

5. When threatened, what did the king do, leading the English Parliament to pass the Declaration of Right, claiming he had abdicated?

6. Although it is also known as the 'Bloodless Revolution', there was bloodshed, with which two nations suffering significant losses?

7. William's side was joined by Protestant volunteers who had fled Catholic France – a group known as what?

8. Three laws that were passed after the revolution in 1689 (the English Bill of Rights, the Toleration Act and the Mutiny Act) collectively committed future monarchs to do what?

9. In 1690, the former king's Jacobite armies met William III's and fought which bloody battle, named after the river near where it took place?

59 Maze

Start at the top and find a path to the middle of the maze.

60   Hillsborough Castle

1. The Classical temple overlooking the lake in the gardens at Hillsborough is named after which Lady Hill?
        a. Beatrice   b. Alice   c. Elizabeth

2. Queen Elizabeth II made her first-ever helicopter journey from Belfast Lough to Hillsborough Castle in 1977, on a visit to mark what important occasion?

3. In 1972, when the role of Governor was made obsolete, Hillsborough became the official residence of which government minister?

4. One of the best-known incumbents to hold this role was the outspoken Marjorie Mowlam. How was she better known?

5. The castle has hosted a number of important negotiations in the Peace Process. In 1985, the Anglo-Irish Agreement was signed by Irish Taoiseach Garret FitzGerald and which British Prime Minister?
        a. Margaret Thatcher
        b. John Major
        c. James Callaghan

6. Hillsborough Castle hosted the negotiations for which landmark treaty in 1998?

7. In April 1999, the Hillsborough Declaration was signed by Prime Minister Tony Blair and which Irish Taoiseach?
        a. Brian Cohen   b. Bertie Ahern   c. John Bruton

8. Why was a round table chosen for the Red Room, which was used for the peace process talks?

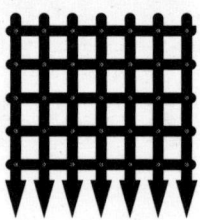

61 Kew Palace

1. Kew Palace's kitchens are remarkably well preserved from Georgian times. The hearth area contains which early gadget, a device for turning a spit by a fly or wheel moved by rising gases in a chimney?

2. The dry larder was used to store dry goods, including expensive aromatic spices. What was the wet larder used for?

3. An early 19th-century bathtub was found in the kitchens, probably used by which royal?

4. Queen Charlotte's Cottage is a small dwelling in the grounds, designed as a rustic escape. It was chiefly used by the family for what?

5. Queen Charlotte was known for her intelligence, and her friends included the novelist Fanny Burney, as well as enthusiastic naturalists Elizabeth Harcourt and Margaret Cavendish, Duchess of Portland. What were these kinds of intellectually minded women known as?
    a. Blue-stockings   b. Lavender-handkerchiefs   c. White hats

6. By 1792, the menagerie in the cottage gardens featured the first of which antipodean animals to arrive in Britain?
    a. Wallabies   b. Wombats   c. Kangaroos

7. What birds were also introduced, which are still to be seen in this quiet area of the gardens?
    a. Partridges   b. Pheasants   c. Grouse

8. The Queen reshaped the cottage gardens inspired by her gardener at Richmond, who was famous for introducing the picturesque landscapes to English aristocrats. Name him.

9. Queen Victoria did what with the cottage and its grounds in 1898, as celebration of her Diamond Jubilee?
    a. Restored them
    b. Opened them to the public
    c. Dedicated them to Albert

62   Kensington Palace – The Sunken Garden

```
A R D N A S S A C M P P N E O
M E R E D N E V A L R M Z S F
S T L C B U A N B N M G Q T E
Q A G D I B G M E T I H W A V
I R B G A A U C A D S S Z R S
I E X U T R A O A O D W Q E I
V N H E M R C U N C I E I N L
D N S H R B D L Y I H E S S L
R U Q E T B L T X E C T S B O
A R T N O U V E A U R P I T M
W B Y U C U L R B A O E C J Z
D B P X R P Y I B E H A R R Y
E U K Z K F O D P L E S A I X
X E U T A T S N X S Q S N S P
I S U B L A F I D A H L I A S
```

- ALCHEMILLA MOLLIS
- ART NOUVEAU
- BRUNNERA JACK FROST
- BUMBLEBEES
- CENTRANTHUS RUBER 'ALBUS'
- CLEMATIS CASSANDRA
- CRADLE WALK
- DAHLIAS
- IRONWORK GATES
- KING EDWARD VII
- LAVENDER
- NARCISSI
- ORCHIDS
- POND GARDEN
- PRINCE HARRY
- ROMNEYA COULTERI
- STATUE
- SWEET PEAS
- TERRACE
- THE MEASURE OF A MAN
- TULIPS
- TURF
- WHITE GARDEN

63 Hampton Court Palace

1. In the Great Hall at Hampton Court Palace, you can still see the entwined letters 'H' and 'A' and an engraved falcon. These are poignant mementoes of which ill-fated woman?

2. Why did Henry VIII and his court of up to 1,000 people have to move constantly between his palaces?
    a. Due to illness
    b. To be seen by different subjects
    c. As they produced too much waste

3. Charles II of England was known to let what kind of animal lie in his bed chamber, which (according to a 17th-century writer) 'made the whole Court nasty and stinking'?

4. What heat-based, curative health treatment did the horses at Hampton Court have access to in the 1860s – before London's humans did?

5. In 1919, 1,800 troops from which army marched through the palace gates and out into Home Park, where they camped for the next two months?

6. What kind of 'feathered' horses are bred at Hampton Court today?

7. How long has it been said to take six gardeners to trim the maze's hedges?
    a. 3 hours   b. 3 days   c. 3 weeks

8. In what year was the palace opened to the public by Queen Victoria?
    a. 1828   b. 1838   c. 1848

9. Approximately how many people visit Hampton Court every year?
    a. 150,000   b. 475,000   c. 1,000,000

64 Maze

Start at the top and find a path to the middle of the maze.

65   Sir Walter Raleigh

Sir Walter Raleigh was an explorer and statesman favoured by Queen Elizabeth I who played a significant part in the colonisation of America.

1. When he was 17 years old, Sir Walter Raleigh fought with the Huguenots in France during the Wars of Religion. What religion were they (and he)?

2. He was famously painted in 1588 with what in his ear?

3. Raleigh also founded a colony in the Americas that he named after the Queen. What is its name?

4. What two crops did Raleigh famously bring back from the Americas?

5. According to myth, what did Raleigh once throw across a puddle?

6. In 1592, when the Queen found out that Raleigh had secretly married one of her ladies in waiting, what did she do?
    a. Imprison them both in the Tower of London
    b. Banish them from the kingdom
    c. Have them placed under house arrest

7. From 1603, Raleigh was imprisoned for treason against James I. While in jail, he made potions from ingredients that he had picked up on his travels, including ambergris. What is ambergris?

8. Raleigh was beheaded in 1618. Legend has it that as a sign of her ongoing devotion, his grieving wife Bess kept what in a red velvet bag until she died 29 years later?
    a. A lock of his hair   b. His teeth
    c. His embalmed head

9. Simon Jones portrayed Raleigh in the 1989 *Potato* episode of which BBC sitcom?

10. Which band sang less than kindly about Raleigh in the 1968 song *I'm So Tired*, due to his popularisation of smoking?
    a. The Beatles   b. The Troggs   c. The Kinks

66 Banqueting House – Interiors and Art

```
P Y R O T C E F E R N F G N S
E R N O I T A C I F I E D O O
D T E Y R U C R E M K P Q I L
A U I W T E S T A M E N T T O
P R A L T F V P A R H L E A M
O R U B E N S N F U D I C L O
T L G N L M A O M C D B N U N
H E U W E K R I E E Z E A C W
E R R H Q M R A T X R R R L R
O U S H A W I T C I Z A E A C
S A V N A C E N M V T L P C H
I L C H Z R U A E O X I M S E
S E Z F F B R W V R A T E I R
E L G A E T N A T S V Y T M U
U I T T U P L X E K N A G U B
```

- ANTWERP
- APOTHEOSIS
- AUGURS
- CANVAS
- CARMELITE
- CHERUB
- DEIFICATION
- EAGLE
- FRETTED
- LAUREL
- LIBERALITY
- MERCURY
- MINERVA
- MISCALCULATION
- OVAL
- PERFORMANCE
- PUTTI
- REFECTORY
- RUBENS
- SOLOMON
- TEMPERANCE
- TESTAMENT
- TITIAN
- URN

67 Palace Lifestyles – Time for Cocoa

1. Chocolate had been highly prized by South American first nations for millennia, but it was first encountered by a European in 1502, when which famous explorer seized a large canoe full of cacao beans?

2. Initially the British saw little value in these beans. When English pirates seized a Spanish cargo in 1579, they assumed they were…
    a. Charred ostrich eggs
    b. Sheep droppings
    c. Large almonds

3. In what year did drinking chocolate finally catch on, with the first London chocolate house luring in Londoners with the promise of an 'excellent West India drink'?
    a. 1557   b. 1607   c. 1657

4. London's hot chocolate shops became known for their gambling and degeneracy. Which of these still exists today as the oldest of London's gentlemen's clubs?

5. By 1690, the royals were hooked. Dedicated chocolate kitchens were built by Christopher Wren as part of which royal palace?

6. At what time of day would King William III and Queen Mary II usually drink chocolate?
    a. Before breakfast
    b. At afternoon tea
    c. At bedtime

7. Thomas Tosier became George I's personal chocolate maker in 1707, but he also ran a chocolate house on 'Chocolate Row' in which London borough?
    a. Greenwich   b. Highgate   c. Hampstead

8. It wasn't until 1847 that which Bristol-based company produced the first solid chocolate bar?
    a. Cadbury   b. Fry   c. Rowntree

68 Crossword

Where Anne Boleyn spent her childhood (2 words)

Across
1. Instances (5)
4. Low noise made by a dog (5)
7. Ability to form mental images of things or events (11)
8. Body of water (4)
11. People or things not already mentioned (6)
14. Intrigue (6)
17. Chest bones (4)
21. Very near in position or character (11)
22. Fashion (5)
23. Country, capital Cairo (5)

Down
1. Cool down (5)
2. Carnivorous marine fish (5)
3. Expressed in words (4)
4. Concession (5)
5. Fruit, an important source of oil (5)
6. Comes down to earth (5)
9. Curve (3)
10. Organ of sight (3)
11. Be indebted to (3)
12. That woman (3)
13. Steal from a person (3)
14. Makes tight against leakage (5)
15. Contented (5)
16. Large northern deer (5)
18. European country (5)
19. Perfume (5)
20. Travel on the back of an animal (4)

69   Banqueting House

1. The Banqueting House is one of the first British examples of which style of architecture?
        a. Palladian   b. Baroque   c. Gothic

2. The exterior of the building was once a colourful mix of honey-coloured and pinkish-brown stone, but it was entirely resurfaced in 1829 with which notable stone from the West Country?
        a. Sandstone   b. Marble   c. Portland stone

3. The hall features a frieze of classical drama masks and garlands of fruit and flowers, reflecting its original use as a theatre. What was the name of the art form performed here in Stuart times, consisting of singing, acting and elaborate special effects?

4. Why did these performances stop after the installation of the Rubens ceiling in 1636?

5. James I is celebrated on the ceiling paintings of the Banqueting House uniting the crowns of England and Scotland. What was his title in Scotland?

6. His son Charles I was executed outside the Banqueting House. In what year?

7. Like his father, Charles II died at the palace; from what natural cause?

8. A Dutch maid accidentally started a fire that destroyed Whitehall Palace in 1698 while doing what?
          a. Heating up an iron
          b. Drying sheets
          c. Smoking a pipe

9. During the fire, what did William III order his staff to do to the Banqueting House, which ultimately stopped it from burning down?

70 Royal History – The Mental Illness of George III

1. In 1788, George III began to experience symptoms, both mental and physical, commonly (and unfairly) referred to as 'madness'. What was the strangest physical symptom?
   a. His hair turned white
   b. His skin turned yellow
   c. His urine was discoloured

2. At which of the surviving royal palaces was he incarcerated?

3. What modern diagnosis has most recently been suggested for Geroge's illness?

4. King George III was given emetics and laxatives, freezing baths and what treatment?

5. After several recurrences of his 'madness', in which year was a regency declared?
   a. 1801   b. 1811   c. 1821

6. The 1994 film *The Madness of King George* was based on the play *The Madness of George III* by which leading British playwright, born in 1934?

7. Why was the title changed for the film version?

8. It won two BAFTAs for Best Film and Best Actor. Which British actor played the king?
   a. Nigel Hawthorne
   b. Jim Broadbent
   c. Nigel Havers

71 Hampton Court Palace – Kitchens and the Tudor Diet

```
R A O B S L Z S A R E I S O T
P T A H T W W N B L O O A T U
S P E L B K Y A E N S N Y S L
O E T C M Y C W I L K O A O Y
P Z Z H A O N S E G D S F U Z
G Y S O L E N R U A P I A R T
D N D C X L R D K Q I N L S T
A S I O C A I S S K G E E C E
N E S L B F S O R A S V D O K
D V I A I C H E E E C W S U C
R L Z T R O U D S V I E B E I
I A Z E Y M B E Z L I Z L R R
D C W R L A R D E R U L A E B
G A M E O T P I A Q A P O R V
E H E A G N Z A R R Y N T S B
```

- ALE
- ALMONDS
- BARRELS
- WILD BOAR
- BOILING HOUSE
- CHARCOAL BRAZIERS
- JOHN BRICKET
- CALVES
- CELLAR
- CHOCOLATE
- BARTHOLOMEW DANDRIDGE
- SOLOMON DE LA FAYA
- GAME
- LAMB
- LARDER
- OLIVE OIL
- OXEN
- PIGS
- PULSES
- SHEEP
- SCOUERERS
- SWANS
- THOMAS TOSIER
- VENISON

72   Lines of Succession

1. The British monarchy is known for being strictly hereditary, but it hasn't always been so. In fact, Henry III became the first English king to inherit by right of being the old king's eldest son in which year?
        a. 1116   b. 1156   c. 1216

2. William I's throne bypassed his oldest son, Robert, who the Conqueror is said to have despised, leading to him being given a nickname meaning?
        a. Red face
        b. Short trousers
        c. Long nose

3. Many people regarded Edmund Mortimer, Earl of March, as Richard II's heir, but when Richard was forced to abdicate on 29th September 1399, the crown went to whom?
        a. Henry IV   b. Henry V   c. Edward II

4. Titulus Regius was a controversial 1484 statute of Parliament that named who as King of England?

5. Parliament drew up the Act of Settlement in 1701, which ruled out which group from becoming monarch?

6. In 1714, George I was chosen for the English throne, skipping around how many people with stronger claims?
        a. 10   b. 30   c. 50

7. The Succession to the Crown Act 2013 is a piece of legislation that ended what?

73 Crossword

One of the most famous diamonds in the world (hyphenated)

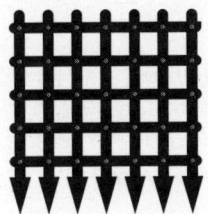

Across
1 Single entities (5)
4 Of a thing (3)
6 Adult female (5)
7 Hire (5)
9 Not a single person (2-3)
10 Front limb (7)
13 Exaggerate, cause to appear greater (7)
15 Turbulent or highly emotional episode (5)
16 Notable or distinctive period of time (5)
17 Light, thin fabric with a wrinkled surface (5)
18 Metal-bearing mineral (3)
19 Structures built by birds (5)

Down
1 Fill with optimism (6)
2 Expand abnormally (5)
3 In the middle of (5)
4 Disguised (9)
5 Free from danger (4)
8 Overbearing pride (9)
11 Seventh letter of the Greek alphabet (3)
12 Infectious disease transmitted by lice (6)
13 Manufacturer (5)
14 Area surrounding the hole on a golf course (5)
15 Extinct bird of Mauritius (4)

74 Kensington Palace

1. George I spent lavishly on new royal apartments for Kensington Palace, creating three new state rooms, the Privy Chamber, the Cupola Room and the King's Drawing Room, which were painted by which artist?
   a. William Sussex
   b. William Cornwall
   c. William Kent

2. Some of the walls and ceilings are decorated with trompe l'oeil paintings. What does 'trompe l'oeil' mean?

3. What is in the centre of the ceiling in the Cupola Room?
   a. Angel   b. Tudor rose   c. Garter star

4. Queen Victoria was born at Kensington Palace in what year?

5. What was unusual about what Victoria was fed as a baby? (A fact that was sufficient enough to warrant a mention in *The Times*.)

6. After her father died, Victoria was brought up under a strict set of rules created by her mother and her mother's advisor, Sir John Conroy. How were these rules collectively known?

7. What was the name of Victoria's canine companion?
   a. Flash   b. Dash   c. Bash

8. Which other British queen was born at Kensington Palace?

75 Palace Gardens

1. Over the years, Kensington Palace gardens have been home to a number of species of plant, including those brought back by plant hunters in the 19th century. *Cornus kousa* is a small deciduous tree delivered by Ernest Wilson. By what English name is it known?
   a. Chilean lantern tree
   b. Chinese dogwood
   c. Chilean myrtle

2. *Trachycarpus fortunei* was another specimen, a tough and hardy evergreen that is native to China, India and Japan. Of what kind of tree is it an example?
   a. Palm   b. Cedar   c. Juniper

3. The *Agave victoriae-reginae* was first brought from Mexico in 1872, and named for Queen Victoria. What type of plant is it?

4. How large are the gardens at Hillsborough Castle?
   a. 50 acres   b. 100 acres   c. 150 acres

5. Which former British politician has some of her ashes scattered in the gardens at Hillsborough Castle?
   a. Mo Mowlam
   b. Margaret Thatcher
   c. Aneurin Bevan

6. Approximately how many pounds of grapes does Hampton Court's Great Vine produce every year?
   a. 200 lbs   b. 400 lbs   c. 600 lbs

7. There are over 12,000 daffodils in the gardens at Hampton Court, but that's only a small portion of how many bulbs overall?
   a. 250,000   b. 650,000   c. 1 million

8. Which new Hampton Court garden was opened by the Duchess of Cambridge (now Princess of Wales) in 2016?

9. Hampton Court is home to a royal park that occupies 750 acres of ancient parkland. What is its name?

76 Royal Dynasties – The House of Stuart

James I was the first Stuart king of England, but he had already been king of Scotland for 36 years as James VI. The House of Stuart went on to rule for over 100 years.

1. What was the name of James I's mother, a great-granddaughter of Henry VII executed in 1586 for conspiring against Elizabeth I?

2. James I's son started the Royal Collection, fathered two kings, and was executed in 1649. Name him.

3. In 1665, what deadly disease struck London during the reign of Charles II, killing 7,000 people a week?

4. James I's wife was Anne of... which European country?
    a. Denmark   b. Norway   c. The Netherlands

5. After his father's death in 1701, James II's son styled himself James III of England and VIII of Scotland. By what name were his supporters known?

6. When Mary II was offered the English throne in 1688, she refused to take it unless...
    a. She got a bigger crown
    b. Her palace was extended
    c. Her husband could rule with her

7. Of what did Queen Mary II die at Kensington Palace on 28th December 1694?
    a. Smallpox   b. Cowpox   c. Chickenpox

8. Following Mary II, her sister, who was never anticipated to take the throne, became queen. What was her name?

9. That queen died without an heir, leaving which royal house to succeed her?

77 Crossword

The last Sikh Maharaja of the Punjab (2 words)

Across

1. Alloy of tin and lead (6)
6. Gas found in air (6)
7. Decree ___, stage in divorce proceedings (4)
9. Compulsion (9)
13. Golden yellow colour (5)
15. Chafe (3)
16. Digit written as VIII in Roman numerals (5)
20. Pre-wedding celebration for men (4,5)
23. Word said at the end of a prayer (4)
24. Slowly, in musical tempo (6)
25. Hitchcock film of 1960 (6)

Down

1. Hit with the fist (5)
2. Large family (5)
3. Loose flowing garment (4)
4. Fruit, a cross between a tangerine and a grapefruit (4)
5. By an unknown author, in short (4)
8. Male offspring (3)
10. Thick sugary liquid (5)
11. Not drunk (5)
12. Swear word (4)
14. Remove from office (4)
17. Country, capital Rome (5)
18. Athletic facility (3)
19. Latin American dance (5)
20. Drench (4)
21. Slightly open (4)
22. At the summit of (4)

78   The Tower Mint

1   The great physicist Isaac Newton worked at the Tower of London as Warden of the Mint, but he is better known for discovering what?

2   In which century was the Mint established at the Tower?

3   Counterfeiting was a huge problem in England. How were forgers punished?
        a. Imprisonment   b. Pillory   c. Execution

4   Until the advent of mechanisation, all coins were handmade. It was hot and dirty work, and loss of what was not uncommon?

5   William Foxley fell into a coma at his workstation, perhaps due to the noxious gases. For how long did he sleep?
        a. 12 days   b. 14 days   c. 16 days

6   Screw-operated presses made life much safer for Mint workers. When were they introduced?
        a. 1680s   b. 1710s   c. 1750s

7   Most of the Mint buildings were situated in the outer ward, which became known as what?
        a. Money Street
        b. Coin Channel
        c. Mint Street

8   For many subjects, coins were the only way that they got to see what?

79 Maze

Start at the top and find a path to the middle of the maze.

80   The Tower of London – The Ravens

```
Y E N E N N I N U M E R E L J
K H E S S E N D N I K N U G O
C U Z L U O Q K K Y B G R J H
O G N U I Y M X C L O I R Q N
R I S K R B S T I F P S D R F
H N K S K I U E H P R U Z K L
L N B T R I R J C F A E Q E A
K L T R B N H X E O B H W R M
L I A P A X Y S E I Q N N O S
E H N F J N S A B I E K I G T
G N E G V X W I G V G E O R E
E E M Z D X N E D G A R D O E
N V O Y I O N C N Q J S O G D
D A I W F G M S L V Y C I E W
Y R D M L E B A M H N B J X G
```

- BRANWEN
- CHICK
- EDGAR
- ERIN
- FALL
- JOHN FLAMSTEED
- FLY
- GEORGIE
- GRIPP
- GROG
- HARRIS
- HUGINN
- KINGDOM
- LEGEND
- MABEL
- MUNINN
- OMEN
- RAVEN
- RHYS
- ROCKY
- SIX
- JUBILEE
- TOWER
- UNKINDNESS

81   **Hillsborough Castle**

1. Since the 1980s, Hillsborough Castle has been the official residence in Northern Ireland for the royal family, but none of them have ever lived there. How many times did Elizabeth II visit?
        a. 25   b. 35   c. 45

2. The castle is colloquially known as 'The Grandest House in County ___'. Fill in the missing word.
        a. Antrim   b. Down   c. Armagh

3. The gardens are known for their collection of trees planted by the royal family. The first was planted in 1928 by Princess Mary (Viscountess Lascelles), the daughter of which king?
        a. George V   b. Edward VIII   c. George VI

4. The latest, planted by Charles III to mark his coronation, was a *Tilia henryana*, which is what kind of tree?
        a. Beech   b. Lime   c. Oak

5. There is an impressive art collection, which has included the work of many well-known names, such as drawings by which 18th-century satirical artist?
        a. James Gillray
        b. Francisco Goya
        c. William Hogarth

6. Works by 18th-century portrait painter George Romney have also been on display. He is known for his artistic muse, Emma Hamilton. She was the mistress of which well-known military figure?

7. The Red Room is home to many small, highly decorative paintings that are densely displayed together in what is known as a what?

8. In the State Drawing Room, there is a 1915 portrait of Winston Churchill engaged in which hobby?
        a. Riding   b. Singing   c. Painting

82   Kensington Palace – The King's Staircase

```
B B E E D A R T S U L A B I J
L U L K N Z C U L R I C U W E
G L T A H P A T S U M O N D B
R I A L O E T E N V J R E B W
E H W H E N P B Z I F E D A I
Y O P D E R A D T Q O B O R L
T U S K E L I Y H D W M O O L
B S A G V H N O O I N A W Q I
N E R W Z J T K U B G H W U A
G M A H O M E T M T D C I E M
U M A N T E R O O M F L G D I
A R B U T H N O T U M Q I S I
R B I H G Z X I I Y R A M W I
D G E O R G I A N M N S N Z M
E C N E S E R P R A R A Y K F
```

- ANTEROOM
- DR JOHN ARBUTHNOT
- BALUSTRADE
- BAROQUE
- ELIZABETH BUTLER
- CHIEF FIRST PAINTER
- DIANA
- GEORGIAN
- GUARD CHAMBER
- MARIE HEDWIG
- HOLKHAM HALL
- WILLIAM KENT
- KING WILLIAM III
- MAHOMET
- MUSTAPHA
- NOTTINGHAM HOUSE
- PETER THE WILD BOY
- PRESENCE CHAMBER
- QUEEN MARY II
- JEAN TIJOU
- ULRIC
- CHRISTOPHER WREN
- WOODEN PANELLING
- YEOMEN OF THE GUARD

83   William Kent

William Kent was an early 18th-century architect, painter and designer who was employed at many of the royal palaces.

1. Born in Yorkshire in around 1685, William Kent showed early promise as a sign painter and was sponsored by local patrons to get an artistic education in which country?

2. In the right place at the right time, Kent got his first royal commission in 1719 when he was hired to paint several rooms in Kensington Palace, by which king?

3. His first work was carried out in the Cupola Room. What is a cupola?

4. The Cupola Room contains an 18th-century musical clock, known as the 'Temple of the Four Great Monarchies of the World'. What are the ancient empires depicted on its four faces?

5. Above it, Kent painted the Garter star. What does this star signify?

6. When the room was finished, the king loved it, while others called it...
   a. A dazzling glamorous fair
   b. A terrible glaring show
   c. An ugly rugged performance

7. Later, George II asked Kent to carry out some work at Hampton Court Palace, too, designing rooms for his son the Duke of Cumberland. For what are these rooms now used?
      a. A residence   b. A gallery   c. A library

8. In 1734, Queen Caroline invited Kent to decorate the stairs to the Queen's State Apartments at Hampton Court Palace. Kent's Roman-inspired setting includes an homage to the Queen, whom he compares to which ancient goddess?
      a. Diana   b. Britannia   c. Athena

84 Maze

Start at the top and find a path to the middle of the maze.

85 Royal Dynasties – The House of Hanover

The House of Hanover succeeded the Stuarts in 1714, ruling for almost two centuries.

1. In 1714, George I acceded to the English throne. What country did he come from?

2. When he arrived in Britain, he quickly became unpopular and was compared to which vegetable?
    a. A carrot   b. A turnip   c. A leek

3. He died from a stroke after eating an apparent excess of what?
    a. Ham   b. Strawberries   c. Cream

4. Who was the last British monarch born outside Great Britain?

5. Known as a bellicose king, George II was also the last British sovereign to do what in 1743 at the Battle of Dettingen in Germany, against the French?

6. George III's reign was defined by a number of wars. While many remember Britain's losses in the American Wars of Independence, they did win which war against the French (1756–63)?

7. Owing to his father's illness, his son George, Prince of Wales (later George IV) took responsibility for the throne in 1811, giving rise to what name for this period?

8. George IV was famously profligate. How much did he spend on his coronation banquet?
    a. £2,500   b. £12,500   c. £25,000

9. George IV's only daughter Charlotte had died in childbirth, and so he was succeeded by one of his younger brothers, the only Hanoverian king not to be called George. What was his name?

86 The Contemporary World of Hampton Court Palace

```
K M P A D A A B T Y R O E H T
F A E G I R H A A A P I F N N
A A L K H M Y G L M I T A T O
R A E S S P A L N F B H Y P S
A I C M B U E M A I P A S D T
D R A K A R F V M I S H H D A
A O E F E H O F L A K T A O W
Y T P D Y U A O R U M U D R C
O C N Y R T B R V A Y O O R T
C I A M F R I D A Y G S W I N
C V L R E E Y N C J U E S T A
T W G A B Z S R A C A F T P E
C A R I B B E A N V I S F T F
G A O S I I I V Y R N E H G E
I K D B R I D G E R T O N O Y
```

- BAMBA MULLER
- BLACK FRIDAY
- BRIDGERTON
- CINDERELLA
- FARADAY HOUSE
- FIRE
- GRACE AND FAVOUR
- HOLMES AND WATSON
- INDIAN ARMY
- LITTLE DORRIT
- MAHARAJA SINGH
- MAMMA MIA: HERE WE GO AGAIN
- ARTHUR CRAIGIE OLIPHANT
- PEACE CONTINGENT
- PIRATES OF THE CARIBBEAN
- SHERLOCK HOLMES: A GAME OF SHADOWS
- SOPHIA DULEEP SINGH
- SOUTH FRONT
- SUFFRAGETTE
- THE PRIVATE LIFE OF HENRY VIII
- THE THEORY OF EVERYTHING
- THE YOUNG VICTORIA
- THREE MEN IN A BOAT
- VANITY FAIR

87 The Field of Cloth of Gold

The 'Field of Cloth of Gold' is the name used to refer to a magnificent spectacle and historic meeting held in 1520 between two European kings, and once great rivals.

1. Name the two kings and former rivals – one of England, one of France – who met during the Field of Cloth of Gold?

2. The English king had once attempted to invade France, in a bid to recreate the glories of his idol, King Henry V. Which Holy Roman Emperor supported his actions?
    a. Frederick III   b. Ferdinand I   c. Maximilian I

3. A treaty of Universal Peace was brokered in 1518, and as a part of this it was decided the two men should meet to affirm their new friendship. Who was responsible for making the English side of the preparations?

4. A neutral location in Calais was chosen for the meeting. Preparations at the site saw hundreds of tents erected and a vast temporary palace constructed, as well as a tiltyard prepared – what was a tiltyard?
    a. Tournament arena   b. Field kitchen   c. Livestock hostelry

5. What did each of the kings agree not to do until they met?
    a. Bathe   b. Shave their beards
    c. Change their attire

6. As the two kings approach, tensions were running high. As they came face to face, each doffed their cap, dismounted their horse, and then what?
    a. Shook hands   b. Sized each other up
    c. Embraced

7. Events across the 18-day spectacular included jousts, tournaments, masquerades and religious services. On the penultimate day, what was seen flying through the sky?
    a. A dragon   b. A pair of doves   c. An eagle

88 Crossword

Kew botanist of George III's social circle (2 words)

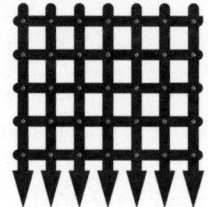

Across

1 Dropped to earth (4)
3 Grown-ups (6)
5 Venomous snake (3)
6 Slightly open (4)
7 Person with special knowledge or skills (6)
9 Seller of smoking requisites (11)
14 Of clothing, off the peg (5-2-4)
18 Protruding abdomen (6)
20 Endorsement made in a passport (4)
21 Decorate with frosting (3)
22 Horny parts of the feet of certain animals, e.g. horses (6)
23 Back part of the neck (4)

Down

1 Praise unduly (7)
2 Immature insect (5)
3 Chimpanzee, for example (3)
4 Divisions of the school year (5)
8 Partly goat, the god of woods and fields (3)
10 Fluffy scarf of feathers (3)
11 Feline mammal (3)
12 Nickname of US President Eisenhower (3)
13 Patio (7)
15 Greek muse of poetry and mime (5)
16 Ask for overdue payment (3)
17 Threaded (5)
19 Male possessive pronoun (3)

89   Royal Events – Coronations

1. Who was the first English monarch to be crowned at Westminster Abbey?

2. After Henry III had the abbey rebuilt, who was the first king to be crowned there, in 1274?

3. Approximately how heavy is St Edward's Crown, used exclusively for royal coronations?
       a. 1.23 kg   b. 2.23 kg   c. 3.23 kg

4. Including the coronation of Charles III in 2023, there have been how many coronations at Westminster Abbey?
       a. 36   b. 40   c. 44

5. Which two English kings did not have a coronation?
       a. Edward V and Edward VII
       b. Edward IV and Edward VIII
       c. Edward V and Edward VIII

6. During the ceremony, the monarch sits on the Coronation Chair, which houses the Stone of Scone, an ancient symbol of monarchy in which British nation?

7. A canopy is held over the sovereign to shield them from the congregation during the most sacred part of the service. What happens at this stage of the ceremony?

8. *Zadok the Priest* is often sung at coronation services. It was arranged by Handel in 1727 for which George's coronation?

9. The singing of what anthem was first included at Elizabeth II's coronation?

90 The Tower of London – The Crown Jewels

1. Comprising more than 100 objects, the Crown Jewels have upwards of how many gems?
     a. 12,000   b. 17,000   c. 23,000

2. The Coronation Regalia are the most famous pieces in the collection, comprising the sovereign's crowns, sceptre, robes, and which other, spherical piece?

3. The gold Coronation Spoon and eagle-headed Ampulla are used for what purpose, the most important part of the coronation ceremony?

4. St Edward's Crown, which is used for royal coronations, had to be remade in 1661 for the coronation of Charles II after what happened to the original?

5. The Imperial State Crown and the Sovereign's Sceptre are set with two diamonds cut from which stone, the largest ever found?

6. Discovered in 1905, the huge stone was cut into nine major stones and 96 smaller gems. How long did it take three polishers working 14-hour days to complete the nine main stones?
     a. 8 weeks   b. 8 months   c. 8 years

7. The Imperial State Crown also features St Edward's Sapphire, said to have been worn in a ring by whom?

8. The Black Prince's Ruby, also set in the Imperial State Crown, is said to have been worn by Henry V during which battle with the French in 1415?

9. The Koh-i-Noor diamond is set in the Queen Mother's Crown. It's said to be unlucky for which people to wear it?

10. The Regalia have been kept at the Tower of London since they were remade for Charles II. Who tried to steal them from the Tower in 1671?
     a. Colonel Blood
     b. Sergeant Sharpe
     c. Admiral Plasma

91 King George III

```
F M U W O O L R E T A W O R K
A W I L L I A M I V T R C N O
F N I F E W U F V Q N B B T Y
J P G F F S G N A P O L E O N
M V S L A R U T L U C I R G A
T X I H I H S O R N Z K W N G
C N A E H C T C H I X P J O U
O I E H G C A W B O X F O R D
H F V M C R R N I N I Q S F W
A E F I E N O A L H K P V O A
N R N D L L E E N N A K Q L L
O I O E O S T R G O F A H K E
V P C G R Z P T F C M R E U S
E M R E M R A F E E R A U Q S
R E T Z G A R E T S E C R O W
```

- ACT OF <u>SETTLEMENT</u>
- ACTS OF <u>UNION</u>, 1800
- <u>AGRICULTURAL REVOLUTION</u>
- <u>ANGLICAN</u>
- <u>AUGUSTA</u> OF SAXE-GOTHA
- BISHOP OF <u>OXFORD</u>
- BISHOP OF <u>WORCESTER</u>
- BUCKINGHAM <u>HOUSE</u>
- CHELTENHAM <u>SPA</u>
- <u>CIVIL</u> LIST
- DUKE OF <u>YORK</u>
- <u>FARMER</u> GEORGE
- <u>FRENCH REVOLUTION</u>
- <u>GEORGE IV</u>
- <u>HANOVER</u>
- HOLY ROMAN <u>EMPIRE</u>
- LEICESTER <u>SQUARE</u>
- <u>MONARCH</u>
- <u>NAPOLEON</u>
- <u>NORFOLK</u> HOUSE
- PRINCE OF <u>WALES</u>
- SEVEN YEARS' <u>WAR</u>
- <u>WATERLOO</u>
- <u>WILLIAM IV</u>

92 Hampton Court Palace – Tudor Food and Feasting

1. Feeding the members of Henry VIII's royal court was a mammoth business. Approximately how many meals had to be cooked each day?
    a. 600   b. 800   c. 1,000

2. Meals were served in 'messes' – portions that would be shared between how many people?
    a. Four   b. Five   c. Six

3. Courtiers were served menus containing approximately how many calories a day?
    a. 2,000   b. 5,000   c. 8,000

4. Why was it considered rude to eat everything on your plate?

5. In the Great Hall, carved and painted heads, known as Eavesdroppers, on the ceiling reminded servants that they shouldn't do what?

6. What was the job of the 'tournebroche'?

7. Approximately how many logs did the kitchens burn in a year?
    a. 730,000   b. 1.3 million   c. 2.3 million

8. Kitchen work made the hearth servants so hot that Henry VIII had to pass rules to stop them doing what?

9. What piece of cutlery was the king the only person to use?

10. How many different meats would a typical feast include?
    a. 15   b. 18   c. 20

93 Crossword

Length of Lady Jane Grey's very short reign (2 words)

Across

1. Block of compressed meat, fish or vegetable extract (5,4)
8. Clan (5)
9. Devoutly religious (5)
10. Period of conflict (3)
11. Character created by Enid Blyton (5)
13. Stage-player (5)
15. Substance used to make cheese (5)
18. Protective garment (5)
20. Dressmaking aid (3)
21. Patriotic (5)
22. Fruit liquid (5)
23. Help yourself, do as you wish (colloquial) (2,2,5)

Down

2. Chinese secret society (5)
3. Not easy to swallow (5)
4. Coconut meat (5)
5. Swell, puff up (5)
6. Having completely lost all heat (5-4)
7. Alienated (9)
12. Performed an action (3)
14. Artificial covering for a tooth (3)
16. Piece of poetry (5)
17. Spread open or apart (5)
18. Former province of western France, on the Loire (5)
19. Remains of buildings that have fallen down (5)

94 Royal Dynasties –
The House of Saxe-Coburg-Gotha

The House of Hanover ended with Queen Victoria and was succeeded by the House of Saxe-Coburg-Gotha.

1. Victoria and Albert, Prince of Saxe-Coburg and Gotha, had how many children?

2. Victoria had which hereditary disorder, leading to the spread of it to many of their descendants around Europe?

3. The reign of Queen Victoria's first son (1901–10) gave the first decade of the 20th century its nickname. Although his family called him Bertie, we know him as who?

4. Due to his mother's long reign, he was heir apparent for how many years?
    a. 39   b. 49   c. 59

5. He earned the nickname Peacemaker after the Entente Cordiale was signed on 8th April 1904 between England and which nation?
    a. Belgium   b. France   c. Germany

6. His son George V was next to rule. Why did he ask his wife to change her name when he became king?

7. George V sailed the world with the Royal Navy. What souvenir did he pick up in Japan?
    a. A jade statuette
    b. One of the crown jewels
    c. A pair of tattoos

8. He was also President of the Royal Philatelic Society, as a result of which of his hobbies?

9. What event led him to decide to change the family name from Saxe-Coburg-Gotha to Windsor in 1917?

95 Charles I's Execution at Banqueting House

```
A R E V I U Q F B V S T V N Y
S L I O F A M S I R A H C I B
C T Y P H O I D P E L G E M E
E L T S A C D E P Y C I E P S
N Q D L O F F A C S K R N E A
S B I N S E C U R E W X I D N
I D I S A S T R O U S R L I E
O G S T E V E I R G K Q M M L
N C T N O S A E R T U X R E U
H A U G H T Y G Q R R Q E N R
P V B P J F N R S I U G F T R
O A B L L E W E R A F Z N V E
W L O O O J O Q K E K C U Q V
E R R W N A D E S M K O D J O
R Y N P I H S R O T A T C I D
```

- ABSOLUTE POWER
- ASCENSION
- CARISBROOKE CASTLE
- CAVALRY
- CHARISMA
- DICTATORSHIP
- DISASTROUS
- DIVINE RIGHT
- DUNFERMLINE CASTLE
- ESCAPE
- FAREWELL
- GRIEVE
- HAUGHTY
- IMPEDIMENT
- INSECURE
- BATTLE OF NASEBY
- OVERRULE
- QUAKE
- QUIVER
- SCAFFOLD
- SEDAN CHAIR
- STUBBORN
- TREASON
- TYPHOID

96   Kensington Palace

1. The statue of Queen Victoria outside Kensington Palace was created by the Duchess of Argyll, who had her studio at the palace, in 1893. How was she related to the queen?
    a. Cousin   b. Daughter   c. Sister-in-law

2. The State Apartments at Kensington Palace first opened to the public on 24th May 1899. How many visitors attended in the first year?
    a. 140,000   b. 240,000   c. 340,000

3. In 1911, the State Apartments at Kensington Palace became the first home of which museum?
    a. The London Museum
    b. The British Museum
    c. The Imperial War Museum

4. From 1922, when she was widowed, Victoria, Marchioness of Milford Haven, moved into a grace-and-favour apartment at the palace, where one of her grandsons was an occasional visitor. Who was he?

5. In the 1960s, the new queen's sister Margaret and her husband Lord Snowdon moved into a private part of the palace. What was his profession?

6. In October 2011, Disney, in cooperation with Historic Royal Palaces, officially crowned its 10th princess at the palace in a ceremony that featured a procession across Hyde Park. Who became the newest princess?

7. Kensington Palace is now whose official London residence?

97 Crossword

Kew has named this type of plant for Queen Victoria (2 words)

Across

1 Highest peak in the Alps, Mont ___ (5)
4 Be in store for (5)
7 Possessed (3)
8 Ordered series (5)
9 Language, jargon (colloquial) (5)
10 Travel on the piste (3)
11 Fastener around which a rope can be secured (5)
14 Beautiful young woman (5)
17 Electronic bleeping device (5)
20 Braid of hair (5)
23 Egg cells (3)
24 Adult insect (5)
25 Step (5)
26 Rug (3)
27 Ned ___, Australian outlaw (1855–80) (5)
28 Bother (5)

Down

1 Fundamental (5)
2 Semi-precious stone (5)
3 Storage box (5)
4 Make an off-the-cuff remark (2-3)
5 Declare invalid (5)
6 Relating to them (5)
12 Field covered with grass (3)
13 Playing card (3)
15 Slippery fish (3)
16 Garland of flowers (3)
17 Stab with a pin (5)
18 Twist into a state of deformity (5)
19 Spacious (5)
20 Flour and water dough (5)
21 Once more (5)
22 Pile fabric used to make bath towels (5)

98   The Masque

Introduced in the 16th century, the masque was an extravagant performance at court in which courtiers and even royals took part.

1. Under which masque-loving Stuart couple did the event become rather an elaborate affair?
    a. William III and Mary II   b. James I and Anne
    c. Victoria and Albert

2. Performed at the Banqueting House designed by Inigo Jones, many of the Stuart masques were created by Jones himself – as set and costume designer – with which renowned poet and playwright as his partner?

3. At the first masque created by the above partnership, the audience was treated to astonishing special effects. These included what scenic wonder?
    a. Artificial clouds that seemed to float
    b. Artificial waves that seemed to move
    c. Artificial trees that seemed to sway

4. As well as elaborate sets, great illumination was required. One 1634 performance alone was said to require how much lighting?
    a. Thirty dozen torches and 50 flambeaux
    b. Seventy dozen torches and 60 flambeaux
    c. Ninety dozen torches and 70 flambeaux

5. The masques featured gods and goddesses, and included a hidden meaning for the audience demonstrating the divine right to rule of the Stuart kings. What is the name of this device?

6. What important part of the event did many in attendance spend weeks preparing and practising for?
    a. The dances   b. A chorus singalong
    c. Their bows and curtsies for the royal family

7. A bizarre tradition at the end of the performance saw the audience upset the table that had been laid out with refreshments. What did this involve?
    a. A food fight   b. Dancing on the table
    c. Smashing glass platters

99 Maze

Start at the top and find a path to the middle of the maze.

100 Queen Charlotte's Cottage

- 18TH CENTURY
- BRICK INFILL
- DUKE OF CLARENCE
- DUKE OF KENT
- FLOWER GARDEN
- KEW PALACE
- NORFOLK REED
- ORIENTAL CATTLE
- ORNE
- PADDOCK
- PICNIC ROOM
- PRINCESS AUGUSTA
- PRINCESS ELIZABETH
- PRINT ROOM
- PRIVY PURSE PAPERS
- REST
- RIVER THAMES
- RURAL
- RUSTIC
- SEDGE
- TARTARIAN PHEASANTS
- THATCHED ROOF
- TIGERS
- WEDDING

101 Royal Events – Jubilee Celebrations

1. Who was the longest-serving British monarch (reigning for 25,782 days), the only one to celebrate a Platinum Jubilee?

2. Just three British kings made it to their Golden Jubilees, and by coincidence they all had the same number in their title. What was it?
   a. II   b. III   c. IV

3. Whose jubilee was celebrated in 1376 with a spectacular week-long joust at London's Smithfield, beginning with a magnificent procession from the Tower of London accompanied by trumpeters?
   a. John   b. Stephen   c. Edward III

4. During prayers at Westminster Abbey for Queen Victoria's Golden Jubilee, what fell upon her bowed head, which observers took as a mark of divine favour?
   a. A white feather   b. A cross   c. A beam of light

5. On 6th May 1935, Queen Victoria's grandson George V became the first monarch to officially celebrate which jubilee?

6. In 1977, Queen Elizabeth II and HRH Prince Phillip made a series of Silver Jubilee tours across Australia, New Zealand and the Pacific Islands, covering how many miles?
   a. 46,000   b. 56,000   c. 66,000

7. What form of transport was used by Queen Elizabeth II during her Diamond Jubilee River Pageant?

8. In 2022, which of the royal palaces was planted with 20 million flower seeds for Superbloom, a new natural landscape designed to benefit pollinators?

102   Hampton Court Palace – Henry VIII

- THOMAS AUDLEY
- ELIZABETH BLOUNT
- CHARLES BRANDON
- LORENZO CAMPEGGIO
- NICHOLAS CAREW
- POPE CLEMENT
- ANNE OF CLEVES
- DUKE OF CORNWALL
- THOMAS CRANMER
- ELIZABETH
- FERDINAND OF ARAGON
- FIDEI DEFENSOR
- HENRY FITZROY
- STEPHEN GARDINER
- HOLY SEE
- CATHERINE HOWARD
- ISABELLA OF CASTILE
- WILLIAM KNIGHT
- MARTIN LUTHER
- MARY
- THOMAS MORE
- PAPAL SUPREMACY
- KATHERINE PARR
- JANE SEYMOUR

103 Queen Charlotte

Queen Charlotte was the loyal and devoted wife of King George III, and Britain's longest-serving queen consort.

1. Queen Charlotte was born Sophia Charlotte of Mecklenburg-Strelitz in 1744, in the north of which country?
   a. Germany   b. Austria   c. Switzerland

2. When she was 17, she came to England to marry 22-year-old George III. How soon after her arrival did they marry?
   a. 6 hours   b. 12 days   c. 24 weeks

3. She gave birth to 15 children, 13 of whom lived to adulthood. Her two youngest sons, Octavious and Alfred, both died after receiving vaccinations against which illness?

4. Queen Charlotte had a wide circle of friends and was close to which French queen?

5. She loved animals and had which pet that was often witnessed grazing outside Buckingham Palace?
   a. A rabbit   b. A sheep   c. A zebra

6. Her husband's mental illness was clearly very distressing. By the time she was 45, what had happened to her hair?

7. Queen Charlotte died in 1818 at Kew Palace after weeks of illness. Where was she buried?

8. When Kew Palace was opened to the public in 1898, who stipulated that the room in which Queen Charlotte died should remain untouched?

9. What is the title of the 2023 Netflix series that is a fictionalised telling of the life and times of Queen Charlotte?

104   Maze

Start at the top and find a path to the middle of the maze.

105   Royal Events – Royal Weddings

1. Whose wedding took place in February 1840 at the Chapel Royal, St James's Palace? (Hint: the bride-to-be proposed.)

2. What flower was in the bouquets of Queen Victoria, Queen Elizabeth II, Catherine, Princess of Wales, and others?
    a. Lavender   b. Orange blossom   c. Jasmine

3. At Queen Victoria's wedding, what weighed in at more than 140 kg (about 22 stone)?
    a. The bride
    b. The floral arrangements
    c. The cake

4. British-made lace for 19th-century royal wedding dresses was sourced from which town in Devon?
    a. Honiton   b. Tavistock   c. Exmouth

5. Prince George (later George V) married Princess Mary of Teck on 6th July 1893, but who had she been intended to marry the previous year?

6. One of the bridesmaids at the wedding of George V's daughter Mary went on to marry Prince Albert, Duke of York, in 1923. What was her name?

7. Which couple married on 20th November 1947?

8. The lace for the wedding dress worn by Catherine Middleton was hand-worked by members of the Royal School of Needlework, based at Hampton Court Palace. Who designed the dress?

106 Hampton Court Palace – Gardens

- ADONIS
- BARGE WALK
- LANCELOT 'CAPABILITY' BROWN
- DAFFODILS
- CELIA FIENNES
- GROTTO
- HOLLIES
- HOME PARK
- ITALIANATE
- LEG OF MUTTON POND
- LONGWATER
- GEORGE LONDON
- MAGIC GARDEN
- DANIEL MAROT
- ROBERT MYERS
- PARTERRE
- QUEEN MARY II'S EXOTICKS
- THE GREAT VINE
- THE KNOT GARDEN
- THE MAZE
- THE TILTYARD
- JEAN TIJOU
- HENRY WISE
- YEW TREES

107 A Royal Christmas

1. In 1304, Edward I wore 'Murrey'-hued robes lined with miniver. Murrey is a dark reddish-purple dye made with kermes, derived from the eggs of the shield louse. What is miniver?
    a. Ferret fur   b. Squirrel fur   c. Pine marten fur

2. In 1532, Henry VIII accepted Christmas gifts from Anne Boleyn, but refused them from whom?

3. On Christmas Day 1286, Edward I's household consumed 13 tuns of wine. How many gallons is that?
    a. More than 1,000
    b. More than 2,000
    c. More than 3,000

4. Queen Charlotte, wife of King George III, started a trend when on Christmas Day 1800 she threw a party for local children that was celebrated around what?

5. One of Queen Victoria's Christmas gifts each year was a huge pie containing what?
    a. 100 birds   b. 100 chocolate coins   c. 100 eels

6. Which Georgian king is said to have been nicknamed 'the pudding king' after his love of plum pudding?

7. What animal arrived in 1255, as a festive gift for Henry III from the French King Louis IX?

8. Who received a 5 cm high edition of Charles Dickens' *A Christmas Carol* for one of her famous dolls houses in 1924?

108 Crossword

Hampton Court is said to be 'haunted' by Jane ___

Across
1 Construction built by a spider (6)
6 Icon representing a person, used in internet chat and games (6)
7 Not in action (4)
8 Legal case (7)
10 Enquire in a meddlesome way (3)
12 Of an egg, fried on one side only, so that the yolk is visible (colloquial) (5,4,2)
15 Named prior to marriage (3)
16 Siberian dog with a thick white coat and a curled tail (7)
19 Underground part of a plant (4)
20 Former name of Chennai, India (6)
21 Wood prepared for use as building material (6)

Down
1 Thin slices of potato fried in deep fat (6)
2 Anne ___, second wife of Henry VIII (6)
3 Ali ___, fictional character who uttered 'Open Sesame' (4)
4 Divisions of a week (4)
5 Tiredness (7)
8 Drivers' resting place (3-2)
9 Eerie, peculiar (5)
11 Flee (3,4)
13 Lay to rest (6)
14 Annoy persistently (6)
17 Vegetable known as lady's fingers (4)
18 Compass point (4)

109   Lady Jane Grey

Lady Jane Grey had an infamously short reign, and for that reason is often called the 'Nine Days Queen'. She was queen from 10th July to 19th July 1553.

1. Who is Lady Jane said to have been named after?

2. What notable woman was her grandmother?

3. At around the age of 10, Jane was sent to live with Edward VI's uncle. Who was he?
    a. Thomas Cromwell
    b. Thomas Seymour
    c. Thomas Cranmer

4. This man married one of Henry VIII's former wives. What was her name?

5. He hoped to make a good marriage match for Jane. On whom did he have his sights?

6. On Edward VI's deathbed, the young king named Jane as his successor. To whom was she married?
    a. Lord Guildford   b. Lord Wrexham   c. Lord Cornwall

7. Once deposed as queen by her powerful cousin Mary, she was convicted of treason. What was her punishment?

8. Jane was executed privately on Tower Green. Although she arrived calmly, what caused her to panic when attempting to locate the chopping block?

9. How old was Jane upon execution?
    a. 15   b. 16   c. 17

110 Palace Servants

1. In Tudor times, servants' food was provided as part of their wage. 'Maides, Servants, Children of Offices, Porters and Skowerers' were given two meals a day of...
   a. Bread, ale and beef or mutton
   b. Sausages, potatoes and mead
   c. Venison stew and water

2. Henry VIII's time was famously unhygienic by today's standards. Servants were encouraged to use what for cleaning?

3. The Groom of the Stool was an important role at court. What was the Groom responsible for?

4. Catalina of Motril was a former servant to Katherine of Aragon. As the queen's lady of the bedchamber, she was asked to testify to what in 1531?

5. What was the chief role of a royal 'wet nurse'?

6. In Irish 'big houses' such as Hillsborough Castle, there were divisions between upper and lower servants, who ate in two different halls. What was the difference between these servants?

7. The servant known as the 'sewer' would wash the royal what?
   a. Toilet   b. Dishes   c. Hands

8. In one census, whose household featured John Brown (54), Personal Servant; Hermann Sahl (49), Librarian; and Lucy Sell (26), a 'Confectionery Maid'?

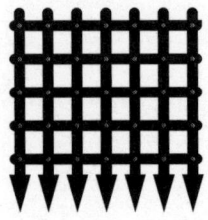

111 Queen Caroline

```
L M L E P A H C J E X G D P F
O A D S E L A W H T E A N L G
N J C T S D R O L A U D N A M
D O I I H X Y V S C N O Y G D
O C G L D G U Q W I T O N H G
N C A P X A U V U L B E V E E
Q H V E A U R A R E U M K E O
R I W R S S P A N D K C Z R R
H J K G L T C A E N I B A R G
C F I A W E H F I W O F U D E
I H C M A N E W S N M C G X I
W Q I I Y A A N J A S L U O I
R B V C T Q U E E N H E S Q I
A S F M A R C H A R L O T T E
H O M D B X J E R S E Y A P Z
```

- AUGUSTA
- AUSTEN
- CARLTON HOUSE
- CHAPEL ROYAL
- CHARLOTTE
- CONNAUGHT HOUSE
- DELICATE INVESTIGATION
- DUKE OF BRUNSWICK
- GEORGE, PRINCE OF WALES
- HANOVER
- HARWICH
- HOUSE OF LORDS
- HYDE PARK
- KING GEORGE III
- LADY JERSEY
- LONDON
- MAJOCCHI
- MARCH OF INTELLECT
- NAPOLEON'S DEFEAT
- PAINS AND PENALTIES BILL, 1820
- PERGAMI
- QUEEN CONSORT
- RADICAL MOVEMENT
- WHIGS

Public Palaces

1. How many palaces are managed by Historic Royal Palaces today?

2. Which is the smallest of these?

3. Which is the oldest?

4. Hampton Court was the first of the palaces to be opened to the public in 1838. By 1881, how many visitors had it received?
    a. More than two million
    b. More than five million
    c. More than ten million

5. Who came to take a last look at the 'Dear Old Palace' the day before Kensington Palace was opened to the public?

6. Why did the government order the closure of the Tower of London, Hampton Court Palace, Kensington Gardens and Kew Gardens in 1913?
    a. The threat of war
    b. An anonymous bomb threat
    c. Suffragette activity

7. Before the Banqueting House was reopened as a historic site in in 1964, which of these was it not?
    a. A military chapel
    b. A military museum
    c. A military barracks

8. Which of the palaces was purchased by the British Government in 1925?

Crossword

An occasion to mark a major milestone in a monarch's reign

Across

1. Pulverise (5)
4. Strike with disgust or revulsion (5)
7. Marked by hard-headed intelligence (6)
9. Ostracise (4)
11. Connected with birth (5)
12. Swollen, tumescent (6)
14. Computer memory unit (4)
16. Make money (4)
19. Fisherman (6)
21. Not fitting closely (5)
22. Produce a sound expressive of relief (4)
23. Digestive fluid (6)
25. Burglar's crowbar (5)
26. Arctic canoe (5)

Down

1. Cause to jump with fear (7)
2. Communion table (5)
3. Strike (3)
5. Pouch used in the shipment of mail (7)
6. Fully developed person (5)
8. With the extremity facing the observer (7)
10. Grass used as fodder (3)
13. Fabric in a plaid weave (7)
15. Set aside for a purpose (7)
17. Line spoken by an actor to the audience (5)
18. Tease (3)
20. Everyone except the clergy (5)
24. Noah's boat (3)

114   Kew Palace – The Great Pagoda

1. The Great Pagoda was built in 1762 by Sir William Chambers for Princess Augusta of Saxe-Gotha-Altenburg, who took charge of developing Kew Gardens when she was Princess of Wales. Why did she never become queen?

2. The pagoda, one of more than 20 original garden buildings at Kew, was said to have been inspired by Chambers' visits to which Asian country?

3. The structure is made of grey brick and is 50 metres high. How many storeys has it?
       a. 8   b. 10   c. 12

4. How many sides has each of these storeys?
       a. 8   b. 10   c. 12

5. How long did it take to complete?
       a. 6 months   b. 6 years   c. 60 years

6. During World War II, the pagoda was put to what use, leading to it falling into disrepair?
       a. A bomb shelter   b. A bomb factory   c. A model bomb test site

7. How much did it cost to build the pagoda in the 18th century?
       a. £2,000   b. £12,000   c. £22,000

8. Eighty of which animal can be found decorating the roofs?

9. When they were replaced during restoration, what modern technology was used to recreate (most of) them?

115 The Tower of London

```
W E Y L T C N S N E Z J M K G
U T C V W A K E F I E L D O A
M I I M I R P V U D T L R M R
O H H Y R R R O N R O R E G R
R W T Y E G P E R I N N A C I
T A O M N L K F I T A C J M S
I S G H Q S S P L G L T A O O
M U D T O Q Y E E U A A R E N
E D B V L A E R L B D T N U N
R B Z B E U I V V L L N E D C
A U R E T E P T S C E O U Q S
Y R U O M R A A A F G W I G G
O Y G K P B A S T I O N L S U
L I B E R T I E S A V I Q L K
E R A L C E D U S J C Z K T J
```

- ARMOURY
- BASTION
- STEPHEN OF BLOIS
- CAEN STONE
- CATAPULT
- CURTAIN
- MARGARET DE CLARE
- DONJON
- GARRISON
- GOTHIC
- GUNDULF
- TOWER LIBERTIES
- MARTIN TOWER
- MENAGERIE
- MOAT
- ROGER MORTIMER
- PORTLAND STONE
- REIGATE STONE
- SIMON SUDBURY
- ST PETER AD VINCULA
- WAKEFIELD TOWER
- PRIVY WARDROBE
- ARTHUR WELLESLEY
- WHITE TOWER

116 Royal Dynasties – The House of Windsor

Anti-German feelings as a result of World War I saw the House of Saxe-Coburg-Gotha change its name to Windsor in 1917.

1 Which monarch was the first Head of the Commonwealth?

2 In which seaside resort did King George V convalesce in 1939 after a serious illness? Clue: it subsequently acquired the suffix 'Regis' (Latin for 'of the King')?

3 What year was 'The Year of Three Kings', when George V died, Edward VIII abdicated and George VI assumed the throne?
    a. 1936   b. 1937   c. 1938

4 Edward VIII gave up the throne for love when he fell for a Catholic divorcee. Name her.

5 Although he inherited the Crown, George VI was forced to buy which two royal residences from Edward VIII, as these were private properties and did not pass to him automatically?

6 Where was Elizabeth II when she found out she was Queen in 1952?

7 What other major world event took place on the day of the Queen's coronation in 1953?
    a. The launch of Sputnik I
    b. The first ascent of Everest
    c. The start of the Vietnam War

117 Crossword

___ House, city in the name of the property that would become Kensington Palace

Across

1 Become broader (5)
4 Country, capital Havana (4)
6 Askew (4)
7 Make reference to (4)
8 Being everywhere equidistant (8)
12 Female relative (4)
14 Native North American tribal emblem (5)
15 Long, detailed story (4)
16 Declare to be a saint (8)
20 Sworn vow (4)
21 Wide-mouthed jug (4)
22 Produced an egg (4)
23 From that time (5)

Down

1 Yarn arranged lengthways on a loom (4)
2 Access into or out of a room (4)
3 Finger-end protector (4)
4 Winter flowering pot plant (8)
5 Warn of danger (5)
9 Primitive chlorophyll-containing, mainly aquatic organism (4)
10 Fastened together (8)
11 Roman language (5)
13 Information reported in the papers (4)
15 Expression of displeasure (5)
17 Yours and mine (4)
18 Islamic republic formerly called Persia (4)
19 Fencing sword (4)

118 Palace Lifestyles – Tudor Medicines

1. Henry VIII liked to make up his own remedies for various ailments. Aside from chamomile, rose and honeysuckle, what was one of the more unusual ingredients found in 'A Pusset Ointment' devised by the king at Hampton Court to heal excoriations'?
    a. Unicorn horn   b. Mermaid scales   c. A lion's claw

2. Some other of Henry's ingredients were actually toxic. For example, 'ceruse' and 'lithage of gold' were both versions of which poisonous metal?

3. 'Violet leaves, apples, mallow flowers, linseed and a newly laid egg' was the recipe for a compound applied to the body on a cloth, a type of treatment commonly known as what?
    a. A compress   b. An ointment   c. A poultice

4. A contemporary medicine, 'Oleum Vulpinum' (a treatment for arthritis, gout and back pain), was oil derived from what animal?
    a. A badger   b. A fox   c. A seal

5. What was regularly done to King Henry's leg ulcers, as doctors believed it was important to keep them open to the air?

6. Which of these is a Tudor 'cure' for a headache?
    a. Drink a medicine made of a mixture of lavender, sage, marjoram, roses and rue
    b. Press a hangman's rope to your head
    c. Give yourself an ice bath

7. 'Hang red curtains around a victim's bed as the red light produced by the curtains will cure the patient.' It is no wonder many died, considering this was thought to be a cure for which deadly disease?

119 Maze

Start at the top and find a path to the middle of the maze.

120

The Palaces Today
(As Seen on Screen… or Not!)

1. The Historic Royal Palaces have appeared as a backdrop in many movies. For example, Hampton Court was used to film which Oscar-winning 2018 movie about the court of Queen Anne?

2. It was also featured in *The Theory of Everything*, a 2014 film about the life of which British physicist?

3. The Tower also appeared in which 2018 film starring Will Ferrell and John C. Reilly as a famous pair of London detectives?

4. Sometimes, other buildings are used to depict the palaces on screen. Ham House stood in for Kensington Palace in which 2009 film starring Emily Blunt?

5. In *The Crown*, Kensington Palace was portrayed by the neo-classical stately home Brocket Hall, home to which two British Prime Ministers in the 19th century?

6. Thame Park in Oxfordshire doubled for which palace in *The Madness of King George*?

7. St Donat's Castle in Wales stood in as shooting locations for both the Tower of London and Hampton Court during the making of which literary Tudor TV miniseries?

8. Despite large parts of the plot being set at Hampton Court, which 1966 Oscar-winning movie about the last days of Sir Thomas More was filmed in a studio?

121 Royal Events – The Palaces at War

1. The Tower of London played a role in training World War I recruits in the Tower moat, including which line infantry regiment of the British Army whose headquarters and museum still exists at the Tower today?

2. The Kew Palace lawn was ploughed up in 1917 and 1918 to grow potatoes for the Home Front. How many tonnes of potatoes were harvested in the summer of 1918 alone?
       a. 22 tonnes   b. 27 tonnes   c. 32 tonnes

3. In 1919, 1,800 soldiers who had fought as part of the British Army camped at Hampton Court Palace as a part of the peace celebrations. By what name were many of these soldiers known?

4. Perhaps Hampton Court Palace's most poignant contribution to the First World War effort was providing the wood that was used to make the coffin for whose burial in Westminster Abbey on 11th November 1920?

5. Kensington Palace was hit by what kind of bomb during the Blitz in 1940, which exploded on the north side of Clock Court?

6. In which palace was the infamous Nazi prisoner of war Rudolf Hess imprisoned in 1941?

7. What was done with the famous Rubens ceiling paintings from the Banqueting House during the Blitz, to save them from bombing?
       a. They were hidden in the basement
       b. They were rolled up and sent abroad
       c. They were cut into smaller sections so that the canvasses could be taken out and stored in a safe place

8. What inflatable obstacles were hoisted over the Tower of London in 1939 to protect the city from low-flying aircraft?

Banqueting House – James I and Anne of Denmark

- KING JAMES BIBLE
- CALAMITY
- CANDLE FIRE
- ROBERT CARR
- COSTUME
- COUNTERBLASTE TO TOBACCO
- DECADENCE
- DENMARK
- DIGNITARY
- DROPSY
- FOOL
- FRIVOLITY
- GUNPOWDER PLOT
- INIGO JONES
- SALON
- SKANDERBORG CASTLE
- SQUABBLE
- STONE OF SCONE
- THE UNDERCROFT
- TORCHES
- VAMPIRES
- GEORGE VILLIERS
- WEREWOLVES
- WITCHES

123 The Royal Collection

1. The Royal Collection is owned by Charles III; in his role as sovereign, he is the custodian of it for the nation. It is managed by which charitable body?

2. The collection contains everything from paintings and sculpture to furniture, carpets, china and ornaments numbering a total of how many items?
    a. More than 500,000
    b. More than 1 million
    c. More than 2 million

3. The collection's paintings include the world's largest and finest holding of work by which 18th-century artist, known for his masterful views of Venice?

4. After Prince Albert's death in 1861, Queen Victoria gave 22 of the best pictures from the Royal Collection to which British museum in his memory?

5. Some of the collection's most dramatic works are a series of giant canvases by Andrea Mantegna, described as 'the greatest masterpieces of the Italian Renaissance outside Italy'. They reside at which of the Historic Royal Palaces?

6. The Royal Collection holds one of the most important Fabergé collections in the world. What decorative objects is Fabergé most famous for?

7. Hillsborough Castle has many Henry Pierce Bone miniatures. The Cornish-born artist was best known for painting on what?

8. The Royal Collection holds a significant number of drawings by Leonardo da Vinci, probably acquired in the 17th century by Charles II and originally bound in one album. How many drawings are there?

124 Maze

Start at the top and find a path to the middle of the maze.

125   Banqueting House – The Rubens Ceiling

As testament to the glory of the Stuart monarchs, the ceiling of Banqueting House by Peter Paul Rubens was commissioned by King Charles I.

1. Rather than painting it on site, Rubens and his assistants painted canvases in his home city and then imported them. What was his home city?

2. The total painted area equals 225 square metres (2,420 square feet), so large that Rubens couldn't fit all the canvases in his studio and had to use additional space in which local buildings?
   - a. A hospital and a zoo
   - b. A stock exchange and a convent
   - c. A school and a library

3. When the paintings arrived, they were found to be the wrong sizes. Why was this?

4. Rubens was given a gold chain and paid £3,000 for his work – what is the equivalent today?
   - a. £158,000   b. £218,000   c. £258,000

5. He never saw his masterpiece in situ, as he was too ill to travel. From what malady did he suffer?

6. One of the paintings represents 'The Union of the Crowns' – of which two nations?

7. In the central scene, on what is James I carried up to heaven?

8. In another scene, the king sits in a setting that flatteringly suggests which biblical king, surrounded by figures that represent abundance and wisdom?
   - a. Solomon   b. David   c. Herod

9. What name is given to the idea that kings are the inheritors of God's power on earth, as depicted in the paintings?

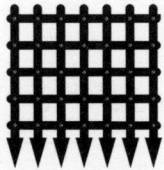

Modern Royals

```
T N O I S S E C C U S O C S W
E V G X C H A R L E S I I I O
R N G E X E S S U S G Q A G R
A A I T O J E G T X I M L L S
G R C T J R E C I A H A L O L
R D H I S N G Z N G T I I U E
A N A D I I D E R E E L M C Y
M A R E R A R U E N D L A E B
I X L W H A B H O L Y I C S E
C E O C Q N H R C M D W S T A
H L T G I F H C L E U G G E T
A A T D T T N S I O I D O R R
E H E N A K R O Y R U R X D I
L K E N I R E H T A C I A G C
K K N A B S K O O R B K S M E
```

- ALEXANDRA
- BEATRICE
- JACK BROOKSBANK
- CATHERINE
- CHARLOTTE
- DUCHESS OF GLOUCESTER
- DUKE OF EDINBURGH
- DUKE OF KENT
- DUKE OF SUSSEX
- DUKE OF YORK
- EUGENIE
- GEORGE
- KING CHARLES III
- LOUIS
- MARIE-CHRISTINE
- MARGARET
- MICHAEL OF KENT
- QUEEN CAMILLA
- RESIDENCE
- RICHARD
- SUCCESSION
- THRONE
- WILLIAM
- KATHARINE WORSLEY

127 Palace Lifestyles – Tudor Sports

1. What type of sport is falconry?

2. Jousting (or tipping) involved two knights on horseback charging at each other and trying to push each other off with a long pole. What was the pole called?

3. What modern sport evolved from the Tudor game of *jeu de paume* ('game of the palm')?
   a. Cricket   b. Rugby   c. Tennis

4. A kind of medieval 'mob football' involved an unlimited number of players on two opposing teams who would try to drag an inflated pig's bladder by practically any means possible to markers at each end of a town. At which annual festival was this sport popular?
   a. Christmas   b. Shrove Tuesday   c. Mayday

5. 'Hastilude' was the name given to different types of what, including jousts, mêlées, quintains and tupinaires?

6. Aiming at 'butts' or 'roving' targets was a feature of which medieval pastime that still exists as an Olympic sport today?

7. Not just a name for a type of sweets, the sport of skittles involved the knocking down of what?

8. One description of young men's amusements in the 1100s describes them as being 'exercised in Leaping, Shooting, Wrestling, Casting of Stones [in jactus lapidum] and Throwing of Javelins.' The casting of stones is said to be the forerunner of which modern sport?

128 Crossword

Someone ruling in a monarch's stead

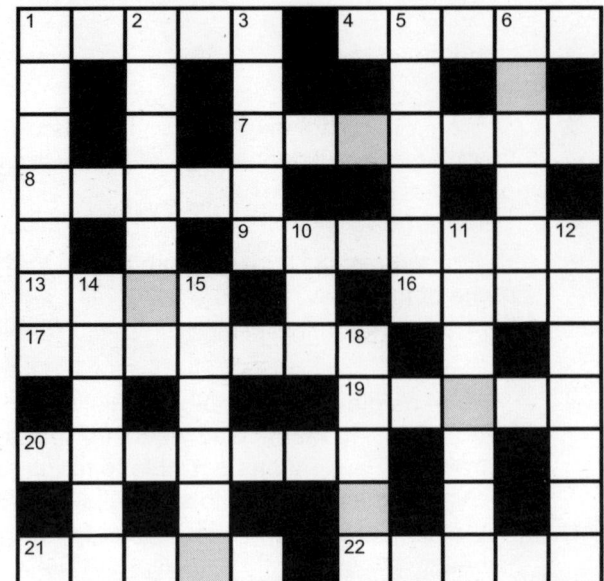

Across
1. Trick (5)
4. Defence plea of being elsewhere (5)
7. Narrow strip of land connecting two larger land areas (7)
8. Criminal who takes property (5)
9. Person who makes garments from animal skins (7)
13. Consequently (4)
16. Fourth largest of the Great Lakes (4)
17. Saved (7)
19. Regenerate (5)
20. Antonio ___, Italian composer and violinist (1678–1741) (7)
21. Subsequently (5)
22. Fearful expectation (5)

Down
1. One more (7)
2. News (7)
3. Steep, high face of rock (5)
5. City in north-east Pakistan (6)
6. Sultanate in north-western Borneo (6)
10. Application (3)
11. Ferrous mineral (4,3)
12. Sequoia (7)
14. Light-sensitive membrane covering the back wall of the eyeball (6)
15. Set of eight notes (6)
18. Lost moisture (5)

129 The Royal Ceremonial Dress Collection

1. Formed in the 1980s, The Royal Ceremonial Dress Collection now has more than 10,000 items housed at which of the royal palaces?

2. One of the oldest items is a red silk hat, associated with which Tudor monarch?

3. Another notable item is the Rockingham Mantua, probably worn by Mary, Marchioness of Rockingham, wife of the British Prime Minister, in the 1760s. The dress required 14 metres of fabric; how wide is it?

4. Brocaded in silver thread and silver lace trim, this impressively wide dress was worn over hoops made from what substance?

5. The Dress Collection is 90 per cent menswear and contains many ceremonial uniforms and accessories, including a fine selection of epaulettes. Where would you wear these?

6. And where would you wear a busby?

7. What was done to Queen Victoria's white cotton drawers to stop them getting lost in the laundry?

8. Before Albert's death, Victoria often chose pastel colours, but afterwards she wore only what colour until the end of her life?

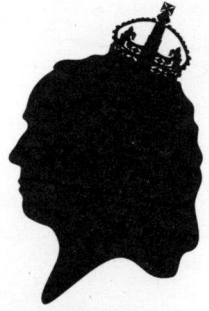

130 Hampton Court Palace – History of the Gardens

1. During Henry VIII's time, the gardens would have included many of which type of garden, characterised by low, overlapping box hedges?

2. Also dating from his reign, the Sunken Pond Gardens would have held what for the court's consumption?

3. The Long Water is a canal commissioned by which king, who ruled 1660–85, in preparation for the arrival of his bride, Catherine of Braganza?

4. William III and Mary II created the Great Fountain Garden on the East Front, which originally contained how many fountains?
    a. 7   b. 13   c. 18

5. Queen Anne planted this garden with many yew trees, which are clipped into what shape?
    a. Hearts   b. Pyramids   c. Ovals

6. The puzzle maze (the oldest existing hedge maze in the world) was first planted in hornbeam, but replanted with which more visitor-friendly shrub in the 1960s?
    a. Oak   b. Yew   c. Elm

7. William III commissioned the baroque Privy Garden of 1701. Why did he never get to enjoy it?

8. In Georgian times, the Kitchen Gardens would produce Grand Sallats (salads) with 'no less than' how many ingredients?
    a. 12   b. 22   c. 35

9. Planted in 1768 by Lancelot 'Capability' Brown, The Great ___ can still be found in Hampton Court's glass house in the Pond Gardens. Fill in the missing word.

131   Hillsborough Castle – The Red Room

```
V H T R A G O H G N I W A R D
B I K S A M A D S K D N F S F
R R E Y N O L D S Y R O Z M M
A C Z G E E F C V K L O Y I O
P O A I R O T C I V G I Y N C
H N P S W O L Z E A N L M I T
A S O Z G E E M S N A A A A G
E O I R Z E A G E D H C L T F
L R L L L R E G E Y S I B U I
M T S B G Y C H L C N T E R D
X S A A Q N A Y A K E I R E U
Y T R P K V E O C Q H L T S B
P E F S P O P N M W T O C O T
T R G S G N I T N I A P N I J
D S G N I T E E M I Y E E S F
```

- ALBERT
- HENRY BONE
- BONE MINIATURES
- CABINET HANG
- CONSORTS
- DAMASK FABRIC
- DRAWING ROOM
- DUKE OF YORK
- ENGLISH SOVEREIGNS
- FAMILY TREE
- HISTORIC MEETINGS
- WILLIAM HOGARTH
- KING GEORGE IV
- MARY MCALEESE
- MARGARET
- PAINTINGS
- PEACE PROCESS
- POLITICAL MEETINGS
- QUEEN VICTORIA
- RAPHAEL
- ROUND TABLE
- SCHOOL OF ATHENS
- SIR JOSHUA REYNOLDS
- ANTHONY VAN DYCK

132   The Tower of London – Escapees

1. The very first prisoner, Ranulf Flambard, Bishop of Durham, escaped from the Tower in 1101 using a rope smuggled to him in what?
   a. A barrel of wine   b. A bag of oats   c. A chamber pot

2. Flambard had formerly been the king's chief minister, with duties including supervising construction projects such as that of what?

3. In 1716, the Earl of Nithsdale was locked in the Tower, sentenced to death for what?
   a. Counterfeiting   b. Murder   c. His part in the Jacobite uprising

4. How did he manage to escape?
   a. By borrowing his wife's clothes
   b. By tying his bed blankets together
   c. By tunnelling out

5. How did oranges and a toothpick help Father John Gerard to escape in 1597?

6. A young Jacobite, George Kelly escaped in 1736 by pretending to have which disorder?

7. The only woman to ever escape, Alice Tankerville was imprisoned for stealing, but managed to get a key to her cell by which method?
   a. Wrapping her gaoler's keys with putty so she could make a copy
   b. Stealing them when he was asleep
   c. Getting him to fall in love with her

8. Two Irish lords, Hugh Oge MacMahon and Cornelius Maguire, escaped after receiving a message with an escape plan hidden in what?
   a. A tin of beans   b. A loaf of bread   c. A bag of sugar

9. A different kind of escape: when Colonel Blood tried to steal the Crown Jewels from the Tower in 1671, he escaped punishment and instead was given what?
   a. A plaster facsimile of the jewels
   b. A country house
   c. A title and acres of lands in Ireland

Solutions

1
1. Ravens.
2. The Tower and the kingdom will fall.
3. a.
4. Beef. Their position in the Royal Bodyguard permitted them to eat as much beef as they wanted from the king's table.
5. A bottle of Beefeater gin.
6. C and R ('Charles Rex').
7. c.
8. Anne Boleyn, Catherine Howard, Lady Jane Grey.
9. b.

2

3
1. Thomas Wolsey.
2. c.
3. a. The kitchens. Bouche of court was food provided as part of a courtier's role.
4. c. The king and the most important guests would enter and leave the palace by barge on the Thames.
5. c.
6. a.
7. The English Civil War. He managed to escape through the Privy Garden… but not for long.
8. b.

4

5
1. b.
2. Normandy.
3. c.
4. Stamford Bridge. There, Harold II killed Harald Hardrada and his own brother, Tostig Godwinson, who supported the Norwegian side.
5. b. The other tactics were used by the Greeks against the Trojans, and the British against the Ottomans.
6. c.
7. He was killed, supposedly with an arrow in the eye.
8. The Bayeux Tapestry.
9. b.
10. c.

6

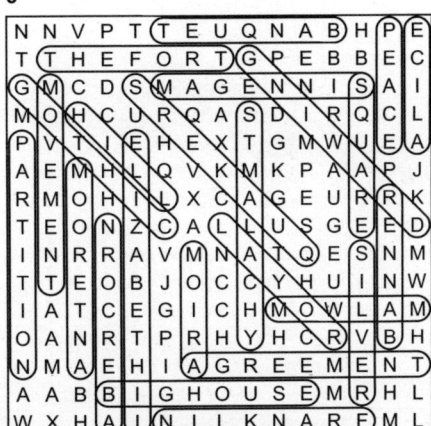

Solutions

7
1. a.
2. b. Dutch House. It has Dutch gables, but Fortrey was actually French.
3. a. It was leased. Queen Caroline leased it to house her three eldest daughters, Anne, Amelia and Caroline.
4. b. George III purchased the freehold for £20,000.
5. b.
6. c.
7. A double wedding to Adelaide of Saxe-Meiningen and Victoire of Saxe-Coburg.
8. 80.

8

HANOVERIANS

9
1. a.
2. Ther own protection.
3. The boys were declared illegitimate.
4. c. Edward's paternal uncle, the Duke of Gloucester. He became Richard III.
5. Smothering the princes with a pillow.
6. Elizabeth of York.
7. b.
8. Westminster Abbey.
9. c.
10. The same paternal uncle, Richard III.

10
1. a. Walter Cromwell was a blacksmith in Putney. He also owned a hostelry, called The Anchor, and was fined by the courts 48 times for watering down his beer.
2. Thomas Wolsey.
3. b. Divorcing his first wife, Katherine of Aragon.
4. b.
5. The translation of the Bible into English.
6. Anne of Cleves.
7. He was imprisoned in the Tower in June 1540 and executed on Tower Hill the following month.
8. *Wolf Hall.*
9. Oliver Cromwell.

11

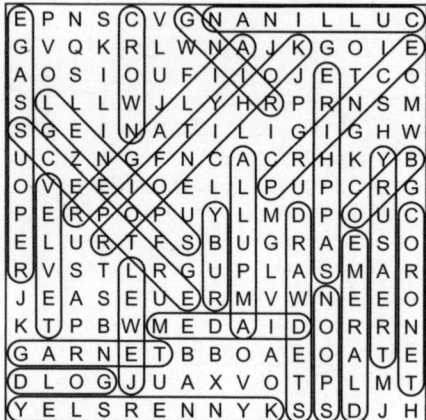

12
1. 4: Anne Boleyn, Jane Seymour, Catherine Howard and Katherine Parr.
2. Henry's brother, Arthur.
3. Because he had sinned in taking his brother's widow, which some scholars believed to be prohibited by the Bible.
4. a. Their marriage was technically bigamous.
5. a.
6. Just over six months.
7. b.
8. They were found guilty of adultery with the king's wife, Catherine Howard.
9. b.

Solutions

13

FARMER

14
1. The Domesday Book.
2. Rufus means red, and he had red hair (and possibly a ruddy face too).
3. a.
4. b. According to legend, he got the blacksmith to put his horse's shoes on backwards to deter any trackers (but luckily the king was so unpopular that no one came for him).
5. a.
6. a.
7. c. The Anarchy (1138–53).

15

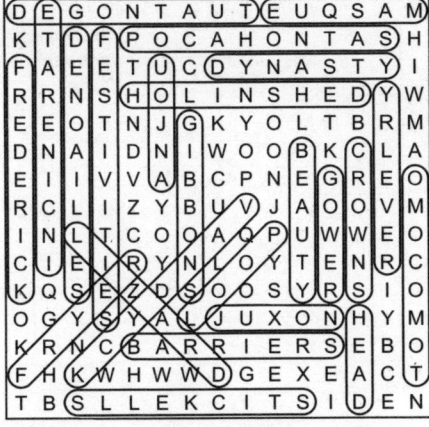

16
1. c. It was known as Nottingham House and still includes a smaller building called Nottingham Cottage.
2. Sir Christopher Wren.
3. a.
4. b.
5. c. Her collection of porcelain with pieces from China and Japan.
6. a.
7. The Orangery.
8. The Serpentine.
9. b.

17

C	R	U	E	T		C	R	E	T	E
A		L		O		O		X		S
R	E	E	F		C	A	B	I	N	S
D		N		C		L		S		A
S	C	U	B	A		F	A	T	T	Y
		M	A	N	M	A	D	E		
T	H	E	T	A		C	O	N	C	H
H		R		R		E		C		E
I	T	A	L	I	C		W	E	E	D
R		T		E		H				G
D	R	E	G	S		J	O	Y	C	E

MARLBOROUGH

18
1. a. Jane Seymour.
2. c.
3. 12.
4. c.
5. Fighting bears.
6. c.
7. a. His life hung in the balance for days, but he did eventually recover.
8. Barnaby was punished.

141

Solutions

19

20

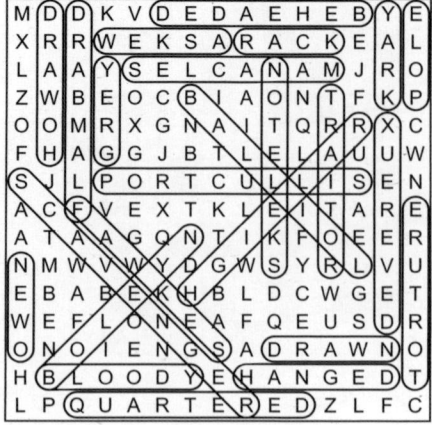

21
1. Viking.
2. b.
3. A rebellion.
4. b.
5. A keep or donjon.
6. a.
7. b.
8. c.

22

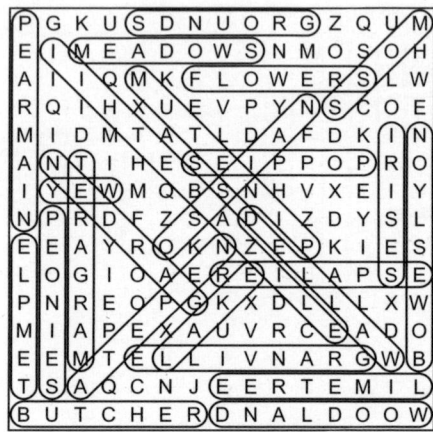

23
1. Henry III ordered it to be whitewashed.
2. Three are square; one is round.
3. To further the suffragette cause.
4. c.
5. A dry defensive ditch, from the Latin *fodere*, to dig.
6. It smelled so bad that it had to be drained by the then Constable of the Tower, the Duke of Wellington.
7. a.
8. The Lion Tower (demolished in the 1800s).
9. b.
10. Some were given to the Zoological Society of London. Others were sold and shipped to America.

24

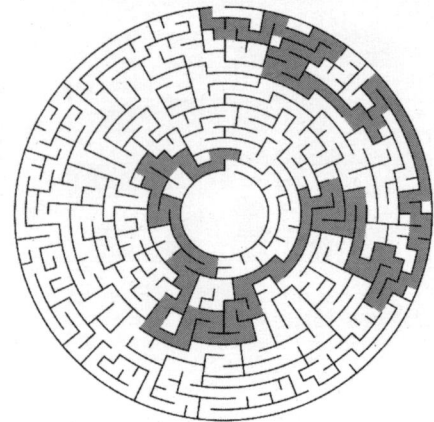

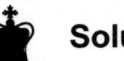 # Solutions

25
1. a. Broom is *planta genista* in Latin, hence Plantagenet.
2. a.
3. The Lionheart.
4. b.
5. Lions.
6. The bubonic plague or 'Black Death'.
7. The Black Prince.
8. The Peasants' Revolt.

26

27
1. Irish Big House.
2. b.
3. a.
4. b. 130 miles from Larne, north of Belfast to Dún Laoghaire, south of Dublin.
5. c.
6. a.
7. Government House.
8. a. Lowering a flag (for the death of President Hindenburg of Germany).
9. Princess Elizabeth, later Queen Elizabeth II. Her aunt was Lady Rose Bowes-Lyons, married to William Leveson-Gower, 4th Earl Granville and Governor of Northern Ireland from 1945–52.

28

V	I	L	L	A		C	U	R	I	E
O			A		D		E			A
T	A	C	T		Y	O	N	D	E	R
E		O	T	T	E	R		U		L
R	U	L	E	R		D	A	N	D	Y
		L		A	L	E		D		
C	L	E	A	N		A	M	A	Z	E
E		A		C	O	L	O	N		T
D	A	G	G	E	R		U	T	A	H
A		U			E		S			O
R	E	E	D	S		J	E	A	N	S

INIGO JONES

29
1. b.
2. The House of Lords, during the opening of Parliament in 1605.
3. James I.
4. Catholic.
5. b.
6. The Tower of London.
7. They were hanged, drawn and quartered. In the end, Fawkes jumped (or fell) from the scaffold before he could be hanged or quartered.
8. The practice of punishing those who refused to attend Anglican services.
9. Burning Fawkes in effigy on Bonfire Night, 5th November.
10. *V for Vendetta*.

30
1. Katherine Parr.
2. Jane Seymour.
3. Catherine Howard. It is said she ran down this gallery to try to find Henry, to beg for mercy when she found out she was going to be charged with adultery.
4. Elizabeth of York.
5. Jane Seymour had been dead for eight years when it was painted.
6. Smallpox.
7. Philip II of Spain.
8. b.
9. More than 2,000.
10. b.

Solutions

31

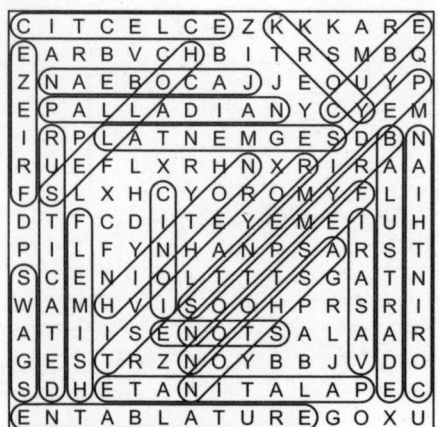

32

1. c. Alexandrina (known to her family as Drina). Victoria was added as a middle name as an afterthought.
2. c.
3. c.
4. Osborne House.
5. *Mrs Brown*.
6. The vote.
7. b.
8. No.
9. c.
10. 'Kaiser Bill', sometimes considered instigator of the First World War.

33

LANCASTRIANS

34

1. John of Gaunt, also known for being Henry Tudor's great-grandfather.
2. a.
3. a.
4. France.
5. a.
6. The Henriad.
7. The House of York.
8. c.
9. He died (in the Battle of Wakefield).

35

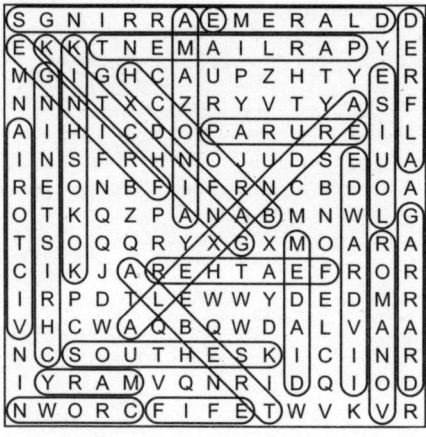

36

1. b.
2. Henry VI. (Since 1923, the Ceremony of the Lilies and the Roses has been held here every year on the evening of 21st May, the day of Henry's death.)
3. A barrel of wine, brandy or rum.
4. Lady Jane Grey. She, her husband and all three Dudley brothers were executed.
5. a.
6. The Ceremony of the Keys.
7. b.
8. c.

Solutions

37

K	E	R	N	E	L		E		V
E		U		A	B	A	C	U	S
B	L	O	G		S		L		I
A		G		S	E	W	I	N	G
B	A	G	E	L		P		P	
		I	T	A	L	I	C	S	
B		N		C		C	H	E	S	S
A	N	S	W	E	R		A		I
D		E		E		S	K	Y	E
G	E	N	I	U	S		E		V
E		G		T	U	R	T	L	E

PETER LELY

38

1 It had one set of defences inside another.
2 a.
3 b.
4 The Royal Mint.
5 c.
6 Prince of Wales.
7 Westminster Abbey.
8 William Wallace.
9 Robert the Bruce.

39

40

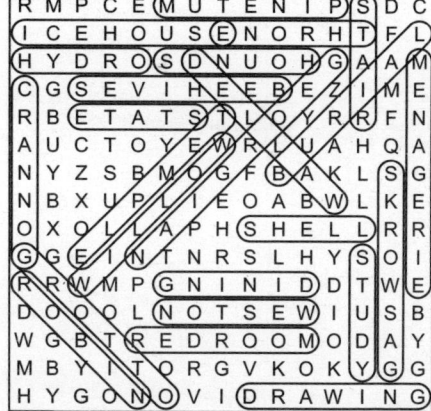

41

1 James I.
2 c.
3 Charles I.
4 Henry VII. He had six tennis courts built, including one at Westminster, and lost £20 by betting on matches (a life's fortune for most people at the time).
5 George III.
6 Queen Camilla.
7 George V.
8 b.

42

(word search grid)

145

Solutions

43
1. a.
2. a. The first English printing press.
3. b. She was one of his subjects, making him the only king not to marry a royal since before 1066.
4. a.
5. Queens' College. The name is intentionally plural.
6. c.
7. a.

44

45
1. Whitehall.
2. Inigo Jones.
3. Cardinal Wolsey.
4. The Cabinet Office.
5. It burnt down.
6. a.
7. 'Maundy'. Royals from Charles II to Queen Victoria gave alms or money to the poor. The day is still sometimes known as Maundy Thursday.
8. a. Feet were apparently pre-washed by servants, echoing how Christ washed the servants' feet at the Last Supper.

46

47
1. Treason.
2. c. He refused to enter a plea, as he believed only God could judge him.
3. c.
4. c. This was so that people would not see him shivering and think it was due to fear.
5. Lord Protector.
6. Puritanism.
7. Christmas.
8. Tumbledown Dick.
9. The Restoration.
10. They dug it up and hanged it at Tyburn.

48

M	A	L	T	A		L	Y	I	N	G
A			R		P		C			R
G	R	O	O	V	E		V	E	T	O
I			O		R		E			U
C	O	M	P	O	S	T	H	E	A	P
		B		S		U		I	N	
H	I	G	H	W	A	Y	C	O	D	E
O			I		D		U			Y
L	E	A	P		E	C	L	A	I	R
L			G		D		A			I
Y	I	E	L	D		D	R	O	N	E

WILLS HILL

Solutions

49
1. Henry VII.
2. Anglesey, in Wales.
3. The Tudor rose. It had both white petals for the Yorks and red for the Lancastrians.
4. Two (Anne Boleyn and Catherine Howard).
5. Hampton Court Palace.
6. b.
7. Bloody Mary.
8. Elizabeth I.
9. b.

50
1. a.
2. b.
3. Mary died. (*Jure uxoris* assumed that a woman's power would be owned and retained by her husband, so the Act was necessary to override this.)
4. a.
5. b.
6. *Three Blind Mice.*
7. Her half-sister, Elizabeth.
8. c.

51

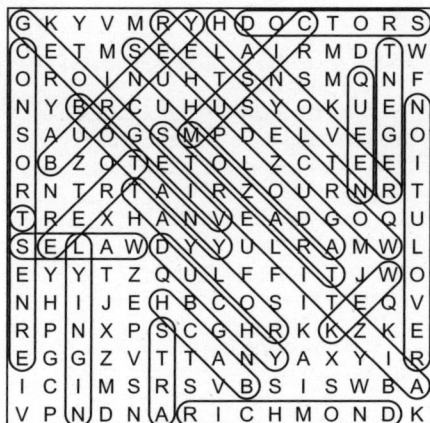

52
1. b.
2. Queen Victoria. One of Sophia's middle names was Alexandrovna, as a tribute to the queen.
3. Suffolk.
4. b.
5. The Census.
6. c.
7. b.
8. Advancement of women.

53

S	Q	U	I	B		S	I	S	A	L
H		S		L		L		T		I
A	R	A	B	I	C	A		A	W	N
R				S		N		M		K
P	I	P	E	S		G	R	I	T	S
		L						N		
W	E	A	L	D		C	H	A	P	S
R		T		U		O				C
A	N	T		S	H	A	M	P	O	O
T		E		T		T		A		N
H	A	R	R	Y		T	E	R	S	E

QUAKER

54
1. Hitler.
2. Reggie Kray.
3. b. One round for every year of her life.
4. Beating the Bounds.
5. Jesus ascending to heaven.
6. His diaries.
7. b.
8. The manacles.
9. The scavenger's daughter.

Solutions

55

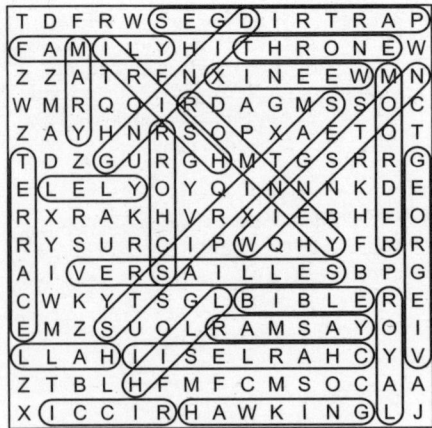

56

1. Visible ageing made monarchs vulnerable, among other reasons.
2. A mixture of white lead and vinegar.
3. Accelerated the ageing process.
4. c.
5. Kohl.
6. b.
7. A dyestuff made of crushed beetles.
8. a. These were soaked in herbs to disguise her foul breath.
9. A creamy drink made from milk mixed with sugar, wine or ale.
10. b. Belladonna juice, which is toxic to humans and would often cause blindness.

57

YORK PLACE

58

1. James II and VII.
2. b.
3. Bring down the Anglican Church and Protestant State.
4. c. James II was tolerated while he had no Catholic heir, but after the birth of his son he was considered too dangerous to rule.
5. He fled London and threw the Royal Seal into the Thames.
6. Scotland and Ireland.
7. Huguenots.
8. Obey Parliament.
9. The Battle of the Boyne.

59

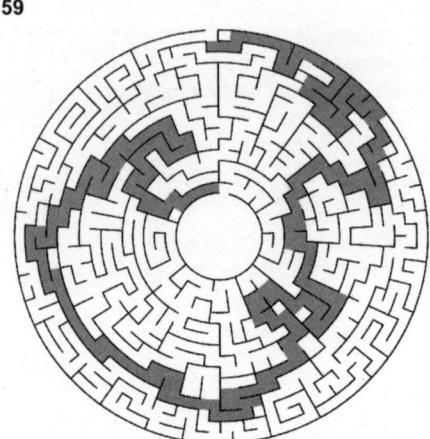

60

1. b.
2. Her Silver Jubilee.
3. Secretary of State for Northern Ireland.
4. 'Mo'.
5. a.
6. The Good Friday Agreement.
7. b.
8. To emphasise equality of all parties.

Solutions

61
1. A smokejack.
2. Storing meat and salted fish.
3. George III, for his medicinal ice baths.
4. Taking tea/having picnics.
5. a.
6. c.
7. a.
8. Lancelot 'Capability' Brown.
9. b.

62

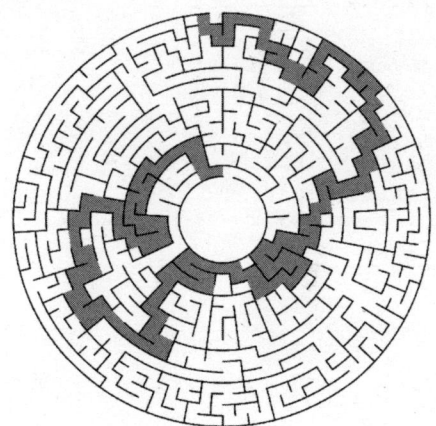

63
1. Anne Boleyn.
2. c. The amount of waste they generated couldn't be cleaned away as fast as they made it.
3. His spaniels.
4. A Turkish bath.
5. Indian. These men who had fought alongside the British Army came for the peace celebrations. Although they arrived too late, separate celebrations were held to honour their fighting and sacrifice.
6. Shire horses.
7. c.
8. b.
9. c.

64

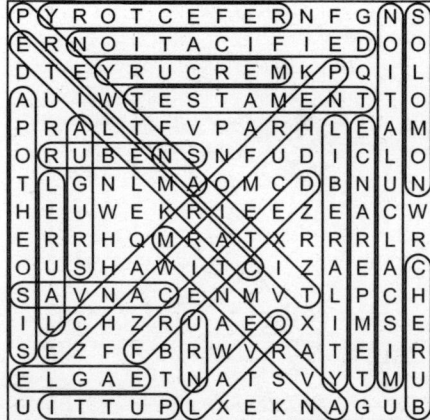

65
1. Protestant.
2. A pearl.
3. Virginia.
4. Potatoes and tobacco.
5. His cloak, so that Elizabeth I wouldn't get her feet wet.
6. a.
7. A secretion from a sperm whale's intestines.
8. c.
9. *Blackadder*.
10. a.

66

 **Solutions**

67
1. Christopher Columbus.
2. b.
3. c.
4. White's.
5. Hampton Court.
6. a. It was served as part of a ritual known as the levee, where the king or queen would get dressed ceremoniously in front of a special chosen few.
7. a.
8. b.

68

HEVER CASTLE

69
1. a.
2. c.
3. Masques.
4. The special effects and lighting involved open flames.
5. James VI.
6. 1649.
7. A stroke.
8. b. She was drying sheets on a charcoal brazier.
9. Brick it up.

70
1. c.
2. Kew Palace.
3. That he suffered from bipolar disorder.
4. Bloodletting.
5. b.
6. Alan Bennett.
7. So that the American audience would know who George III was.
8. a.

71

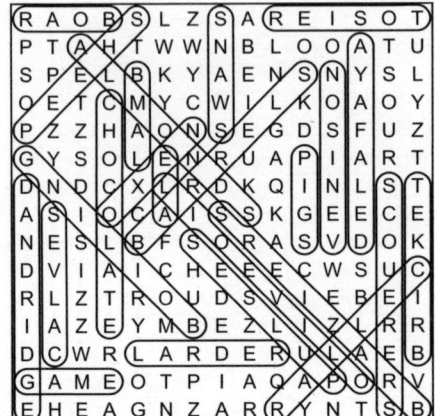

72
1. c. He was only nine years old.
2. b. He was called Robert 'Curthose', from the Norman-French word *courtheuse*, meaning 'short stockings' or trousers.
3. a. Henry Bolingbroke (Henry IV).
4. Richard III.
5. Catholics or their spouses. Even today, a British monarch may marry a Catholic, but not be one.
6. c. This was because he was a Protestant.
7. The system of male primogeniture, under which a younger son can displace an elder daughter in the line of succession.

Solutions

73

U	N	I	T	S		A		I	T	S
P				W	O	M	A	N		A
L	E	A	S	E		O		C		F
I		R		L		N	O	O	N	E
F	O	R	E	L	E	G		G		
T		O		T				N		T
		G		M	A	G	N	I	F	Y
D	R	A	M	A		R		T		P
O		N		K		E	P	O	C	H
D		C	R	E	P	E				U
O	R	E		R		N	E	S	T	S

KOH-I-NOOR

74

1. c.
2. Optical illusion; it's French for 'deceive the eye'.
3. c.
4. 1819.
5. The Duchess chose to breastfeed, an unusual choice for royals at the time, who ordinarily employed a wet nurse.
6. The Kensington System.
7. b.
8. Queen Mary, wife of King George V.

75

1. b.
2. a.
3. Succulent.
4. b.
5. a.
6. c.
7. c.
8. The Magic Garden.
9. Home Park.

76

1. Mary, Queen of Scots.
2. Charles I.
3. The Plague.
4. a.
5. Jacobites.
6. c. Her husband became William III.
7. a.
8. Anne.
9. Hanover.

77

P	E	W	T	E	R		U		A
U			R		O	X	Y	G	E	N
N	I	S	I		B		L		O
C		O	B	S	E	S	S	I	O	N
H	O	N	E	Y		O		A	
	U			R	U	B		T	
	S		U		E	I	G	H	T
S	T	A	G	P	A	R	T	Y		A
O		J		T		A	M	E	N
A	D	A	G	I	O		L		G
K		R		P	S	Y	C	H	O

DULEEP SINGH

78

1. Gravity.
2. 13th.
3. c. Forgery was considered treason and so punishable by death.
4. Fingers and eyes.
5. b. Even King Henry VIII came to poke the man, who eventually woke and lived for another 40 years!
6. c.
7. c.
8. What the monarch looked like.

Solutions

79

80

81
1. a.
2. b.
3. a.
4. b.
5. c.
6. Lord Nelson.
7. A 'cabinet hang'.
8. c. He took up the hobby later in life and was captured by his art tutor, Sir John Lavery.

82

83
1. Italy.
2. George I.
3. A rounded dome forming or adorning a roof or ceiling.
4. Assyria, Persia, Greece and Rome.
5. Membership of the Order of the Garter.
6. b. With its painted pilasters, marble chimney piece and gilded lead statues, it must have looked quite garish.
7. b. The Cumberland Art Gallery, which exhibits paintings from Historic Royal Palaces and the Royal Collection.
8. b.

84

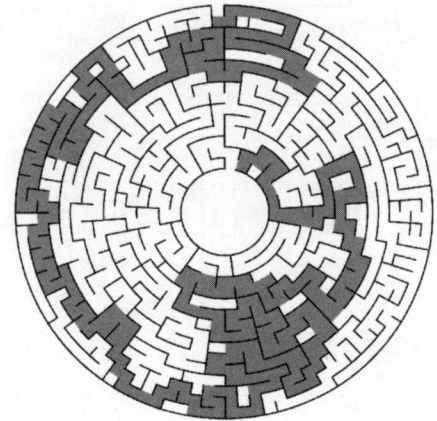

Solutions

85
1. Germany. He spent much of his reign absent as he was homesick for Hanover, and he never bothered to learn English.
2. b.
3. b.
4. George II.
5. Fight side by side with his soldiers (at the age of 60).
6. The Seven Years' War.
7. Regency.
8. c. He spent £25,000, when a family could survive on £30 a year.
9. William IV.

86
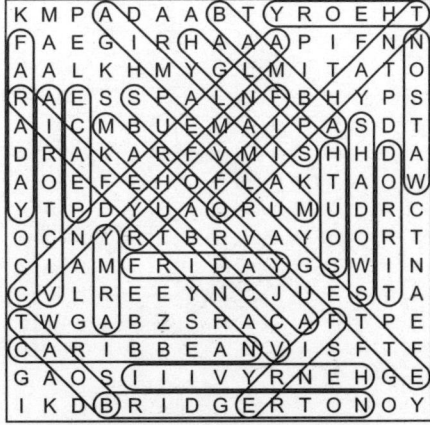

87
1. Henry VIII and François I.
2. c.
3. Cardinal Thomas Wolsey.
4. a.
5. b. Though Henry did not stick to this agreement.
6. c. The men embraced like brothers before walking arm-in-arm to their meeting.
7. a. This 'dragon' kite was tethered to a carriage and intended to represent François's salamander and Henry's Welsh Tudor dragon. Eyewitnesses claimed it hissed and its eyes glowed, indicating it was possibly filled with fireworks!

88

JOSEPH BANKS

89
1. William I.
2. Edward I.
3. b. 2.23 kg equates to nearly 5 lbs.
4. b. Including the double coronation of William III and Mary II.
5. c. Edward V (believed to have been murdered in the Tower of London together with his younger brother Richard of Shrewsbury, Duke of York) and Edward VIII (who abdicated before he was crowned).
6. Scotland.
7. The sovereign is anointed with holy oil.
8. George II.
9. *The National Anthem*.

90
1. c.
2. The Sovereign's Orb (its cross is a reminder that sovereign power comes from God).
3. Anointing the monarch with oil.
4. It was destroyed (melted down) by Parliamentarians after the execution of Charles I.
5. Cullinan (Cullinan I is known as the Great Star of Africa).
6. b.
7. St Edward the Confessor. It was discovered in his tomb in 1163.
8. Agincourt.
9. Men.
10. a.

Solutions

91

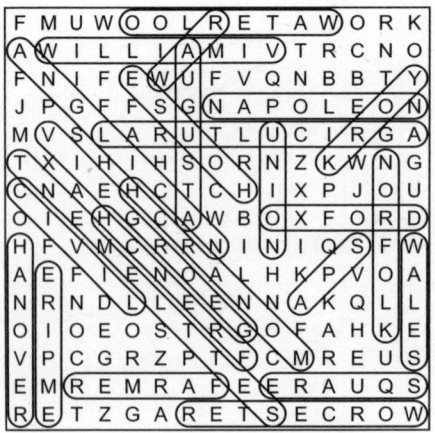

92
1. b. Around 400 courtiers were entitled to two meals a day.
2. a.
3. b.
4. The leftovers were an important source of food for the poor.
5. Gossip.
6. Turning meat on spits.
7. b.
8. Cooking 'naked, or in garments of such vileness as they do now, nor lie in the nights and days in the kitchen or ground by the fireside'.
9. A fork.
10. c. Among other meats, a feast included beef, venison, veal, pheasant, heron, bitterns, gulls, larks, swan and rabbits.

93

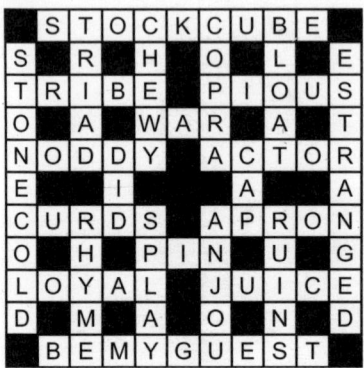

NINE DAYS

94
1. Nine.
2. Haemophilia.
3. Edward VII.
4. c. The longest time as heir apparent, apart from that of Charles III.
5. b.
6. Her name was Victoria Mary, but he didn't think she should be called Queen Victoria, so she became Queen Mary.
7. c. These were a tiger on one arm and a dragon on the other, said to symbolise the west and east.
8. Stamp collecting.
9. Anti-German feeling during World War I.

95

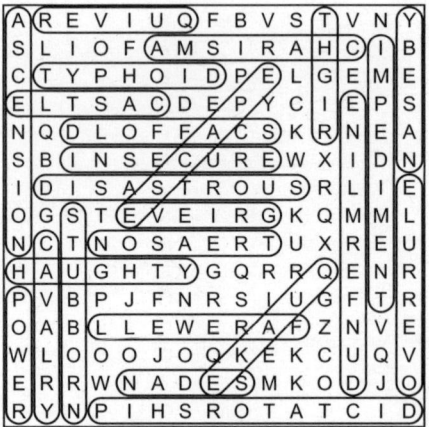

96
1. b. Also known as Princess Louise, she was one of Victoria's daughters.
2. c. There were 340,000 visitors in the first year – more than in any single year in the following century.
3. a. It was then called 'The London Museum', a name it has now reclaimed.
4. Prince Philip.
5. Photographer.
6. Rapunzel.
7. The Prince and Princess of Wales (William and Catherine).

Solutions

97

B	L	A	N	C		A	W	A	I	T
A		G		H	A	D		N		H
S	C	A	L	E		L	I	N	G	O
I		T		S	K	I		U		S
C	L	E	A	T		B	E	L	L	E
		E		C				E		
P	A	G	E	R		P	L	A	I	T
R		N		O	V	A		G		E
I	M	A	G	O		S	T	A	I	R
C		R		M	A	T		I		R
K	E	L	L	Y		A	N	N	O	Y

GIANT WATERLILY

98
1. b.
2. Ben Jonson. Their partnership was fraught with quarrelling as each felt their contribution more important.
3. b.
4. c.
5. An allegory.
6. a.
7. c. It was an act they were said to participate in with 'great glee'.

99

100

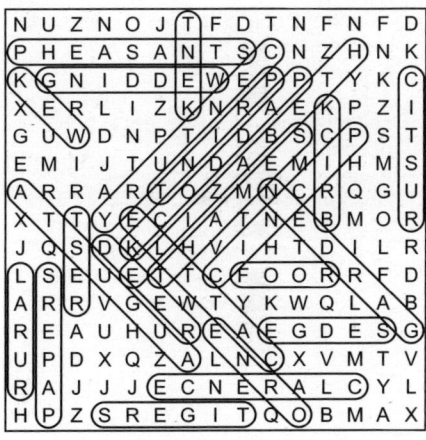

101
1. Elizabeth II.
2. b. Edward III, Henry III and George III all clocked up more than 50 years on the throne.
3. c.
4. c.
5. A Silver Jubilee. These were not officially celebrated prior to this date.
6. b.
7. Boat. Tthe royal barge was one of 1,000 boats in a very rainy flotilla.
8. The Tower of London. The seeds were planted in the moat for Elizabeth II's Platinum Jubilee.

102

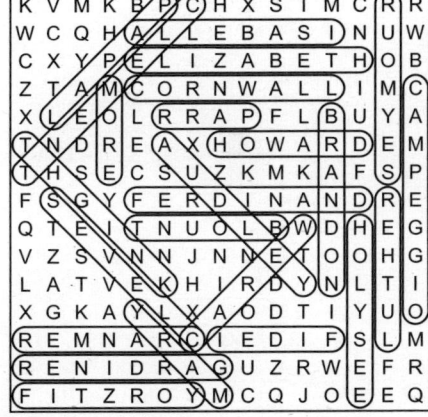

Solutions

103
1. a.
2. a.
3. Smallpox.
4. Marie Antoinette. Charlotte prepared lodgings for the French royal family should they need to flee, but she was later distraught to learn that the King and Queen of France had been executed.
5. c.
6. It had turned white.
7. St George's Chapel, Windsor Castle.
8. Queen Victoria.
9. *Queen Charlotte: A Bridgerton Story*.

104

105
1. Queen Victoria. She had to propose as she had the higher status.
2. b.
3. c. Many smaller cakes were also baked, so that pieces could be sent to hundreds of people.
4. a.
5. His brother Albert, who died of influenza.
6. Lady Elizabeth Bowes-Lyon, later known as the Queen Mother.
7. Princess Elizabeth and Prince Philip.
8. Sarah Burton at Alexander McQueen.

106

107
1. b. From its winter pelt.
2. His wife, Katherine of Aragon.
3. c.
4. A decorated yew tree.
5. a. In a tradition that continued into the 1930s, a large woodcock pie was sent each year to the sovereign by the Lord Lieutenant of Ireland.
6. George I.
7. An elephant.
8. Queen Mary.

108

SEYMOUR

Solutions

109
1. Jane Seymour.
2. Mary Tudor, the youngest sister of Henry VIII.
3. b.
4. Katherine Parr.
5. His nephew, the future king, Edward VI.
6. a.
7. Mary was merciful. Jane and her husband were allowed to remain at the Tower of London as high-status prisoners. But they were ultimately executed.
8. She had blindfolded herself. She was reported to shout, 'What shall I do? Where is it?' before someone stepped in to help.
9. c.

110
1. a.
2. Their own urine.
3. Toileting needs. They were responsible for cleaning up, monitoring bowel movements and liaising with the Royal Doctor about the king's digestive health – a highly sought-after role as the Groom also shared the king's confidences.
4. That Katherine had consummated her marriage to Henry's older brother, Arthur.
5. Breastfeeding.
6. Upper servants were English or Protestant; lower were Irish and Catholic.
7. c.
8. Queen Victoria's, as per the 1881 census.

111
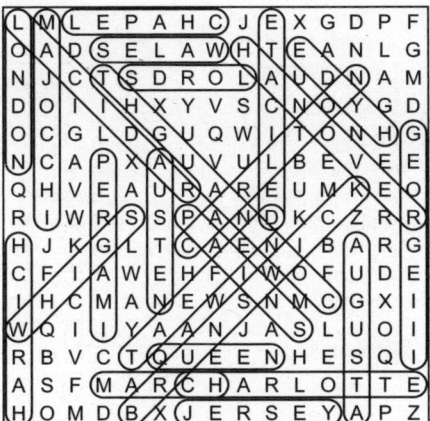

112
1. Six.
2. Kew Palace.
3. The Tower of London (parts date back to the 11th century).
4. c.
5. Queen Victoria. Kensington Palace was opened to the public in 1899.
6. c. Because of suffragette activity, in particular Leonora Cohen's attack on the Crown Jewels.
7. c.
8. Hillsborough Castle.

113

JUBILEE

114
1. Her husband (Prince Frederick) predeceased his father (George II).
2. China. Chambers described it as an imitation of a Chinese Taa. It has been described as 'the most important surviving chinoiserie building in Europe'.
3. b.
4. a.
5. a.
6. c.
7. b.
8. Dragons.
9. 3D printing. Eight dragons are carved from cedar; the remaining 72 were 3D printed.

Solutions

115

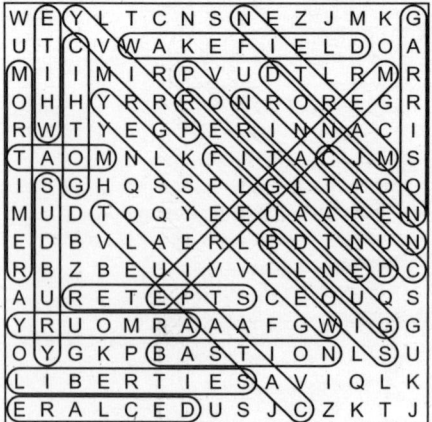

116

1. George VI.
2. Bognor.
3. b.
4. Wallis Simpson.
5. Balmoral Castle and Sandringham House.
6. At Treetops Hotel in Kenya.
7. b.

117

NOTTINGHAM

118

1. a. 'Unicorn horn, one ounce'. In actual fact, the substance was taken from a narwhal's tusk.
2. Lead.
3. c.
4. b. 'Take a whole Foxe, except the bowels, and put hym in a vessel, and powre uppon him Welle water, and salte Water, [and] old oyle.' Bullein's *Bulwarke of Defence against Sickness and Disease* (1562).
5. Lancing.
6. c.
7. Smallpox.

119

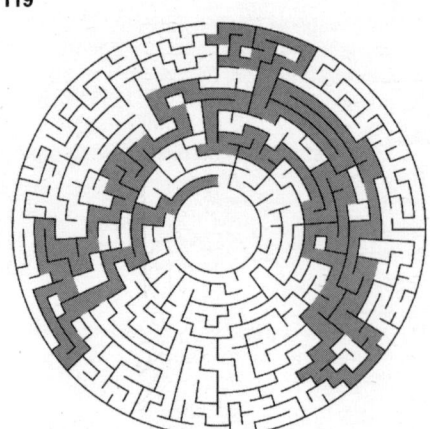

120

1. *The Favourite*.
2. Stephen Hawking.
3. *Holmes and Watson*.
4. *Young Victoria*.
5. Lord Melbourne and Lord Palmerston.
6. Kew Palace.
7. *Wolf Hall*.
8. *A Man for All Seasons*. It won the 1967 Oscar for Best Picture.

 # Solutions

121
1. Royal Fusiliers.
2. b.
3. Gurkhas.
4. The Unknown Warrior. The wood came from an oak tree in Home Park. This unidentified soldier was given a state funeral to represent the gratitude of all to the many thousands who gave their lives.
5. An incendiary bomb.
6. The Tower of London.
7. c.
8. Barrage balloons.

122

123
1. The Royal Collection Trust.
2. b.
3. Canaletto. George III bought 52 of Canaletto's best oils and a significant body of his drawings in 1762.
4. The National Gallery.
5. Hampton Court Palace.
6. Imperial Easter Eggs.
7. Enamel.
8. 600.

124
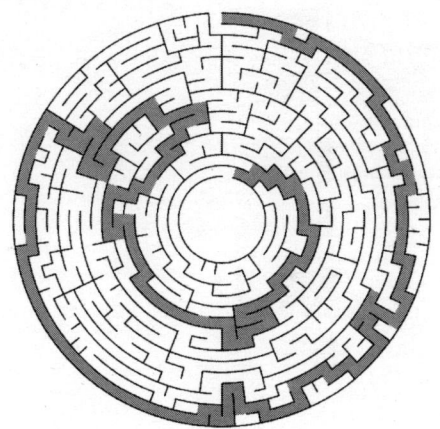

125
1. Antwerp.
2. a.
3. Belgian and British imperial measurements were different.
4. b.
5. Gout.
6. England and Scotland.
7. The wings of a huge eagle.
8. a.
9. The divine right of kings.

126
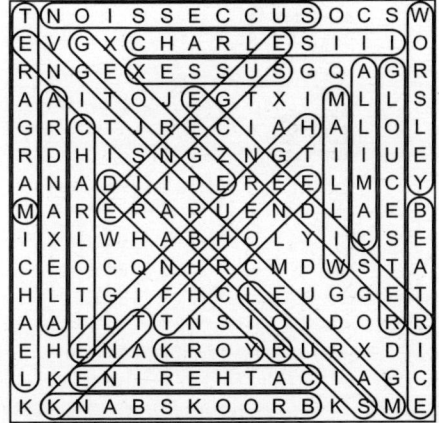

 **Solutions**

127
1. A method of hunting small mammals using hawks, falcons and other birds of prey.
2. A lance.
3. c.
4. b.
5. Duels or mock battles.
6. Archery.
7. Pins – usually nine of them.
8. Lawn bowls.

128

REGENT

129
1. Hampton Court.
2. Henry VIII.
3. Over 2 metres.
4. Whalebone.
5. On your shoulders.
6. On your head.
7. They were numbered.
8. Black.

130
1. Knot garden.
2. Freshwater fish.
3. Charles II.
4. b.
5. b.
6. b.
7. He died in 1702, from complications after falling off his horse and before the garden was finished.
8. c.
9. Vine.

131

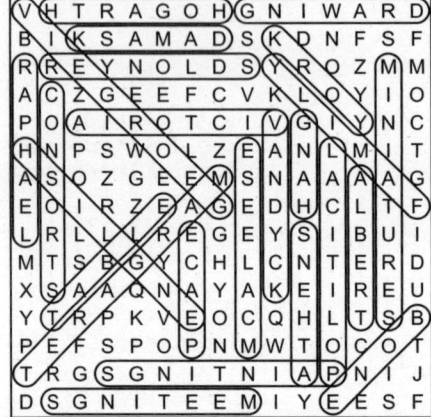

132
1. a. He used the wine to get his gaolers inebriated.
2. Fortifications.
3. c.
4. a. By borrowing his wife's clothes (although both alternative methods were used successfully by others).
5. He used them to write a secret note in invisible ink (before abseiling down the walls to his waiting friends).
6. Asthma.
7. c. She was then captured and manacled at the waterline to drown.
8. b.
9. c.